on file

£3.75

NOF

(Farries)

SEMINAR STUDIES IN HISTORY

The Decline of
the Liberal Party
1910–1931

D1514163

SEMINAR STUDIES IN HISTORY

A full list of titles in the series
will be found on the back cover
of this book.

SEMINAR STUDIES IN HISTORY
General Editor: Roger Lockyer

The Decline of the Liberal Party 1910–1931

Paul Adelman

Reader in History,
Kingston Polytechnic, Surrey

LONGMAN

LONGMAN GROUP UK LIMITED
Longman House
Burnt Mill, Harlow, Essex, CM20 2JE, England
and Associated Companies throughout the World.

First published 1981
Seventh impression 1990

Set in 10/11 pt. Baskerville, Compugraphic

Produced by Longman Group (FE) Ltd
Printed in Hong Kong

ISBN 0-582-35327-0

British Library Cataloguing in Publication Data

Adelman, Paul
    The decline of the Liberal party, 1910–1931 –
    (Seminar studies in history).
    1. Liberal Party – History
    2. Great Britain – Politics and government
    – 1910–1936
    I. Title   II. Series
    324.24106'09   JN1129.L42

    ISBN 0–582–35327–0

Contents

Acknowledgements

We are grateful to the following for permission to reproduce copyright material:

Hutchinson Publishing Group Ltd and the author's agents for an extract from *Lloyd George – A Diary* by Francis Stevenson, published by Hutchinson.

The cartoon on the cover appeared in Punch on 20 February 1918.

Seminar Studies in History

Founding Editor: Patrick Richardson

Introduction

The Seminar Studies series was conceived by Patrick Richardson, whose experience of teaching history persuaded him of the need for something more substantial than a textbook chapter but less formidable than the specialised full-length academic work. He was also convinced that such studies, although limited in length, should provide an up-to-date and authoritative introduction to the topic under discussion as well as a selection of relevant documents and a comprehensive bibliography.

Patrick Richardson died in 1979, but by that time Seminar Studies series was firmly established, and it continues to fulfil the role he intended for it. This book, like others in the series, is therefore a living tribute to a gifted and original teacher.

Note on the System of References:
A bold number in round brackets (**5**) in the text refers the reader to the corresponding entry in the Bibliography section at the end of the book. A bold number in square brackets, preceded by 'doc' [**docs 6, 8**] refers the reader to the corresponding items in the section of Documents, which follows the main text.

ROGER LOCKYER
General Editor

Foreword

After years of decline and disunity in the later nineteenth century, the Liberals achieved a remarkable electoral victory in 1906, winning 400 seats and an overall majority in the House of Commons of 130. The government that was then formed, was arguably the most brilliant and constructive of the twentieth century, especially after Asquith became Prime Minister in 1908, and it dominated the political life of Edwardian England. But the great ministry of Asquith, Lloyd George and Churchill, proved to be England's 'last Liberal Government'. By 1918 Liberal unity had vanished; by 1924 the reunited Liberal party consisted of only forty MPs; at the general election of 1935, after a decade of rapid political change, they were down to twenty-one MPs. Since the Second World War they have failed to reach even that figure, though it is fair to add that the number of their elected representatives does not reflect their voting power in the country at large.

The aim of this study is to consider how and why this transformation took place during the key years which lie between the political crises of 1910 and 1931. It is a story which is bound to fascinate the historian. For the decline of the Liberal party represents one of the great tragic themes in modern British politics; the supersession in the 1920s of a party which was born in the age of Palmerston, and whose history encapsulates much of the public life of later Victorian and Edwardian England. It involves the clash of powerful and outstanding political personalities, such as Asquith and Lloyd George, and the drama of great events in wartime and in time of peace. It also represents in some sense the decline of an ideal of moderation and rationality in politics which goes back perhaps to the eighteenth century. Liberal decline is also indissolubly linked with another major theme of twentieth-century British history – the rise of the Labour party.

Even before the Second World War the subject had already engendered a mass of biographical and autobiographical material which, with the notable exception of Lord Beaverbrook's *Politicians and the War* (17), was inferior both as history and literature. It is only in the last twenty years or so that the problem of the decline of the Liberal party has become the subject of serious academic study, and that for two reasons. The private papers of the leading politicians of the period – most notably those of Lloyd George – have now become available to the professional historian; and, with the passage of time, the passions and acrimony of an earlier period of historical debate have largely passed away, and it is possible to adopt a more dispassionate view of the events and personalities of the age of Liberal decline. It has meant, for example, that earlier views of Lloyd George have been modified as a result of the writings of historians like A. J. P. Taylor (**11**), Kenneth Morgan (**81, 108**), John Campbell (**98**) and John Grigg (**100, 101**).

It is largely on their work and that of other present-day historians that this short study is based. Indeed, I have deliberately tried to concentrate on those incidents and topics which have become the focal points for discussion or controversy in recent historical writing. The purpose of this book is therefore simply to introduce the student to a central and compelling theme in modern British political history and to some of the outstanding historical work which it has inspired.

For the sake of uniformity, in referring to the principal opposition party, I have employed the term 'Conservative' throughout, though 'Unionist' was normally used until after 1922.

Paul Adelman

Part One: The Crisis of Liberalism

1 Liberalism under Strain 1910–14

A new phase began in the history of the Liberal government of 1906 with the emergence of the constitutional crisis over the powers of the House of Lords. As a result of the Lords' rejection of Lloyd George's 'People's Budget' in November 1909 in an act of suicidal folly, the ending of their absolute veto over Commons' legislation, which had been used with such blatant partisanship during the past three years, became inevitable. In the general election fought on this issue in January 1910 the enormous Liberal majority of 1906 was cut down by some hundred seats, and Asquith became leader of a minority government; but he was able to carry on as Prime Minister with firm support from Labour and the Irish. In April the Commons passed three famous resolutions, the most important of which stated that a Bill passed by the Commons in three successive sessions should become law despite the opposition of the Lords. This became the basis of a Parliament Bill, and shortly afterwards the Lords, resignedly, passed the Budget.

Yet it took the government another exhausting and depressing year, marked by the death of Edward VII, and a further general election which was virtually a re-enactment of the first, before Asquith could obtain from the new sovereign, George V, those secret 'guarantees' involving the creation of Liberal peers, which he now believed were vital to his task. That alone would make it possible to checkmate the Conservative majority in the House of Lords if they chose yet again to defy the will of the Commons and reject the proposed Parliament Bill. The Bill easily passed through the Lower House in June 1911, and was finally debated in the House of Lords in a broiling August in an atmosphere of mounting tension and excitement. There, the majority of Conservative peers, the 'Ditchers', led by the aged Halsbury, decided to oppose the Bill, even after the revelation of the King's firm commitment to create enough Liberal peers if necessary to get it through. 'The question is,' said Lord Selbourne, a leading Ditcher, 'shall we perish in the dark, slain by our own hand, or in the light, killed by our enemies' (66). In the end, the 'Hedgers', the small group of moderate Conservative peers led by Curzon and Lansdowne, realising the futility of resistance, were able to whip up enough support for the government to get the Bill passed by the narrow majority of seventeen. In this way the long-drawn-out constitutional crisis came to an end, though its short-term consequences were to plague the Liberals until the outbreak of the First World War.

It left the government 'exhausted but unable to rest' (*35*), beset with problems much more serious than had faced it in its conflict with the House of Lords. On the very day that George V gave his approval to the new Parliament Act, 18 August 1911, the country was faced with its first national railway strike, an indication of the new spirit of 'labour unrest' and trade union resurgence, which seemed to typify the four years preceding the First World War. Labour unrest was marked by major industrial disputes between 1910 and 1912 on the railways and in the mines and docks over pay, conditions, and (for the railwaymen and dockers) union recognition as well, disputes which spilled over into other industries up to 1914. Contemporaries were alarmed not only by the extent of strike action (more days were lost through strikes during these years than at any time since the 1890s) but also, in the words of a recent historian, by its 'violent, unofficial and insurgent character' (*33*). This was seen in the legendary rioting at Tonypandy in November 1910 during the bitter South Wales coal strike, the prelude to the national strike of 1912; and in the sporadic looting and rioting in some of the ports during the dock strikes of 1911–12. Moreover, the temper of the industrial movement of the period seemed to many Edwardian men of property to smack of the revolutionary syndicalism preached by its main exponent in England, Tom Mann, who was certainly active as a strike leader in the docks during these years. These fears were given credence also by the publication in 1912, by a group of Welsh miners, of the most famous of British syndicalist pamphlets, *The Miners' Next Step*, and the formation a year later of the Triple Alliance of miners, railwaymen and dockers to coordinate industrial action.

In addition to this unprecedented outburst of industrial unrest after 1910, the government was tormented by the outbreaks of Suffragette militancy organised by the formidable and publicity-conscious Mrs Emmeline Pankhurst and her daughters, through their Women's Social and Political Union, founded in 1903. Their campaign began after 1905 in a fairly moderate way with the interruption of Liberal political meetings and the harassment of ministers, in an attempt to coerce the government into granting 'Votes for Women'. In the years following the rejection of the Franchise Bills of 1912 (which allowed the possibility of female franchise) it reached a new crescendo of violence and hysteria marked by arson, outrage and attacks on property (*47,*

48). The government replied with the harsh and distasteful weapons of imprisonment, forcible feeding, and the 'Cat and Mouse' Act. Yet however embarrassing and irritating the Suffragette campaign was to Liberal ministers, it remained to all of them, even to the most sympathetic, like Grey and Lloyd George, a peripheral issue. This was not true of the last and most difficult of the problems that faced them before August 1914, that of Ireland.

In 1912 the Liberal government, committed in principle to the granting of Home Rule for Ireland and dependent after 1910 on Irish Nationalist votes in the House of Commons, introduced its Home Rule Bill. This was a moderate measure, similar in many respects to Gladstone's Bill of 1893 and, like its predecessor, based on a policy of Home Rule for *all* Ireland. But in the intervening period the divisions between Catholics and Protestants in Ireland had hardened; and the Liberals now found themselves opposed by the united stubborn resistance of the Ulster Unionists, prepared to push their opposition – as the formation of the Ulster Volunteers soon showed – to the point of armed revolt. In this they were in effect backed up by the Conservative Party in Britain, who were tempted to use Ulster extremism, as they had once tried to use the Lords, to destroy the hated Liberal government. 'I can imagine no length of resistance,' said Bonar Law, the Conservative leader, in July 1912, 'to which Ulster will go, which I shall not be ready to support' (**31**). This and similar sentiments expressed by Irish Unionist leaders like Carson were denounced by Asquith as a 'Grammar of Anarchy'. But Anarchy (as the Suffragette campaign had also shown) was not something that Asquith could either comprehend or master. Faced with intransigence and subversion by the Unionists both at Belfast and at Westminster, and unwilling or unable to impose a more compromising policy upon his Irish Nationalist allies, Asquith adopted his old policy of 'Wait and see'. By a display of 'massive calmness' (in his admiring biographer's phrase) and the conviction that the Irish question remained a suitable case for parliamentary treatment, the Prime Minister hoped to bring his opponents to their senses (**103**). Yet the ultimate effect of this policy of 'drift' was to exacerbate rather than relieve the growing tensions in Ireland, tensions which were bound to increase anyway during the two-year waiting period, between the introduction of the Home Rule Bill and the moment when in 1914 – the Lords having exhausted their powers of rejection under the new Parliament Act – it would become law. Hence these years saw a mounting menace in Ireland: the formation of private armies north and south of the border, the growing grip on the province of the Ulster Unionist Council, the Curragh 'Mutiny', and the Larne gun-running incident which so inflamed Catholic opinion. By July 1914 the country had been brought to the verge of civil war.

In March, however, bowing to harsh facts, Asquith had offered the opposition an Amending Bill which would have postponed the application of Home Rule to Ulster for six years. This was dismissed by Carson as merely 'a stay of execution'. Nevertheless, the party leaders made one final if half-hearted effort to agree on a solution at the Buckingham Palace Conference held in July. This was, almost inevitably, a failure, and with its collapse and Britain's entry into the First World War about a week later, the Irish constitutional problem was shelved for the duration.

These crises that dominated the history of the Liberal government between 1910 and 1914 have been seen by one distinguished historian as a period of 'domestic anarchy' (**31**); another writer, George Dangerfield, regards them as marking the 'Strange Death of Liberal England' (**66**). The latter, in his influential book with this title, argued that during these years the old Liberal values of toleration, moderation and reason, bruised and battered even in 1906, were mercilessly done to death by an unholy alliance of peers, suffragettes, syndicalists and Unionists, linked only by their hatred of Liberalism and commitment to unreason and extremism, and the result was that 'by the end of 1913 Liberal England was reduced to ashes'.

But in terms of historical analysis, without underestimating the seriousness of the problems that faced the Liberal government during these years, it is as well to see them in less dramatic and more realistic terms, as problems not essentially different in kind from those that have faced nearly all peacetime governments in this country from Gladstone onwards (**59, 73**).

From this point of view it cannot be said that the government's record was wholly unsuccessful or, from a party point of view, demoralising. The outcome of the Lords' crisis was ultimately victory for the Liberals, particularly for Asquith who, in the later stages at least, displayed superb parliamentary mastery and control. It is true that in his attitude towards the Suffragette campaign the Prime Minister showed the other side of his political character: a timidity and condescension, an inability to respond imaginatively to what Gladstone earlier called a 'virtuous passion' which infuriated his feminist opponents at the time and has been condemned by their supporters since. Yet, in terms of maintaining party unity and pushing through the Liberals' programme after 1910, a case can be made for Asquith's reluctance to give priority to the franchise issue. (**80**). However misguided the government's motives may have been and however illiberal their methods, the militant Suffragette campaign *was* contained during this period without, as far one can tell, having any disastrous effects on the Liberal party itself or its electoral support.

A similar point may be made about the effects of the 'labour unrest'. Whatever the causes of strike action or the fears of middle-class opinion about the spread of syndicalism as a contributory factor, for the government it was an intrusive practical problem because of the disruptive effects that protracted strikes in the railway or coal industries particularly would have on society and the economy. Hence the government's policy when faced with such industrial action was one of cautious intervention, aimed at bringing about negotiations between the two sides, compromise and a speedy settlement.

Lloyd George was the main instrument of this policy, partly because of Asquith's ineptness in dealing with trade unionists compared with the Welshman's negotiating skill and sympathy with the working-men. In 1907, when he was still at the Board of Trade, Lloyd George had achieved a brilliant coup by settling the railways dispute. Now, in 1911, as Chancellor of the Exchequer, by a similar mixture of threats and soothing syrup, he was able to get the railwaymen to call off their strike after only two days. It was Lloyd George too who was heavily involved in the settlement of the miners' strike the following year by his support for the Miners Minimum Wages Act (**95**). It is true that these settlements were purely *ad hoc* and temporary; and, as far as the miners' was concerned, largely fraudulent. Nor did they imply any clear conception by the Liberals of the role of the state in industrial disputes; no attempt was made to intervene, for example, in the London dock strike of 1912. Nevertheless, in the short run the government coped with industrial unrest reasonably successfully.

The Liberals' greatest failure by 1914 was over Ireland. Even here, owing to the grim luck of the outbreak of the First World War, the government was able to stop the slither towards anarchy in Ireland, at least temporarily. What would have happened if Britain had not entered the war, with the support of both Irish Nationalists and the Unionists, it is difficult to tell. It is possible that in the end some compromise solution on the lines of Asquith's 'Exclusion' policy of 1914 might have been accepted.

The real barometer of the success or failure of Edwardian Liberalism lies perhaps not with these prewar crises, but in the cold record of electoral statistics. In 1906 the Liberals achieved a landslide victory, winning 400 seats and an overall majority of 130. Their Labour allies achieved 30 seats in the House of Commons, while the Conservatives lost more than 200 seats and were reduced to 157 MPs. What was especially significant in the results was that the Liberals not only regained 'traditional' seats in the 'Celtic fringe', the industrial North, and parts of the Midlands lost in the later nineteenth century, but also made inroads into the Conservative heartland in the South, and, for the first time, won over industrial Lancashire and many working-class areas of London. The general election of 1906 thus marked a profound shift in the political geography of Liberalism (91), a shift which was to be modified but not substantially altered by the elections of 1910.

Those elections were largely fought, as Asquith intended them to be, on the symbolic issue of House of Lords reform, an issue which he felt would rally all the anti-Conservative forces to the government. In this he was successful. The result of the 1910 elections was that the Liberals lost more than 100 seats and, with 272 MPs after December 1910, were reduced to exactly the same total as the Conservatives in the House; only support from Labour and the Irish enabled them to continue as the governing party. Thus the great Liberal tidal wave of 1906 receded drastically in 1910, though not back to the low-water mark of 1900 (22). Though the middle classes, especially in southern England, returned to the Conservative fold as a result of their fears of 'Lloyd Georgeism', the new gains made by the Liberals in the industrial North and the poorer areas of London, were largely retained; and this represented a working-class vote *for* radicalism (61, 43). Hence, P. F. Clarke argues, the elections of 1910 mark the emergence of 'class politics' (i.e. working-class recognition of the primacy of social and economic issues) which had been gradually building up in the early twentieth century, and was emphasised in 1910 by the profound electoral gulf between the Liberal North, Scotland, and Wales, and the Conservative South (25). It was this new outlook, he contends, that drove the urban working classes towards the Liberal party, with which Labour was associated as a junior partner in a 'Progressive Alliance'; and it was on this electoral base that Edwardian Liberalism could continue to thrive.

Nevertheless, between 1910 and 1914 the Liberal party was faced with an insidious decline in terms of by-election results. During these years the Liberals lost fifteen seats to the Conservatives, and won two from Labour. Most of these were lost in straight fights with their main opponents; but – a particularly worrying feature for the Liberal leaders – the Labour party put up third-party candidates in eleven constituencies, and five Liberal seats were lost due to this intervention. This reflected the growing breakdown of the Lib/Lab alliance at grassroots level, particularly in industrial Yorkshire and the mining areas of South Wales, much to the distress of Ramsay MacDonald, its main architect and supporter on the Labour side. By the eve of the First World

War, the Miners' Federation of Great Britain was planning to sponsor twenty-one Labour candidates against the Liberals (**29**); one recent estimate suggests that the Labour party would have fielded between 150 and 170 candidates at the next election, compared with seventy-eight (in January 1910) its highest pre-war total (**39**). Moreover, the profound social and economic changes taking place beneath the surface of late-Edwardian society were bound, so it has been argued, to lead to Labour advance and Liberal decline (**87**).

Whatever truth there may be in this thesis so far as general trends are concerned, it is difficult to argue that *electorally* Labour was effectively challenging Liberalism for the working-class vote during this period. In the elections of 1910, Labour found it virtually impossible to win seats against the Liberal Party in the handful of constituencies where it dared to challenge them: none of the forty seats won in January and only two of the forty-two seats won in December, were gains from Liberals (**60, 22**). Labour finished bottom of the poll in all twelve by-elections it fought between December 1910 and July 1914, and the highest percentage of votes it obtained was thirty per cent (**71**); it also lost four seats, two to the Liberals. It is true of course, as McKibbin has argued in detail, that three of these losses were due to the stubborn links with Liberalism that persisted in miners' seats in the Midlands (Hanley, Chesterfield, North-east Derbyshire); that the verdicts were close in many of the by-election results; and that Labour's overall vote *was* increasing compared with 1910 (**39**). Nevertheless, it is difficult to fault Clarke's conclusion: 'There is . . . plenty of evidence that Labour could embarrass the Liberals. But whereas in the 1900 . . . and in the 1906 parliament it had snatched by-election victories, after 1910 the Labour party seems to have run out of steam. There is nothing to suggest that it was moving into a position to win further seats in its own right' (**60**).

From the electoral point of view it is clear that the Liberal party *was* facing serious difficulties before 1914, due more to a resurgence of the Right at both local and national level than to the rise of the Left (**62**). But though the Liberals might have lost the next general election if peace had prevailed, especially if the Lib/Lab alliance collapsed, there is little hard evidence that the Liberal party was dying or even in decline during this period. Nor can this conclusion be deduced from the state of the government itself [**doc. 1**]. There were profound clashes of personality within the Cabinet, and strong differences of opinion over such issues as the House of Lords, female suffrage, and, especially, the naval estimates – the latter worsened by Churchill's brashness at the Admiralty. But these were no more, and perhaps rather less, if the evidence of the Crossman Diaries (**112**) is anything to go by, than faces many contemporary governments. Moreover, Asquith did have the capacity to smooth over differences and reconcile divergent interests among his still formidable team (**75**). The best testimony to his government's essential harmony and his own mastery lies in the fact that before August 1914 there was not one resignation, despite Morley's twenty-three attempts! As Grey wrote to Lloyd George in June 1913: 'There is one great abiding cause of satisfaction in having been in this Cabinet – we have been in it 7 ½ years and I believe it can be said with truth that the personal relations of all of us have not only stood the long strain but have gained in attachment . . .' (**90**). Thus, despite occasional mutterings and gossip, there was no real challenge to Asquith's leadership; certainly not from Lloyd George, between whom and the Prime Minister there was mutual respect and admiration. Together, 'they provided a massively effective partnership' (**84**).

In the summer of 1914, compared with the pessimism of Labour and the negativism of its Conservative opponents, the Liberal government still gave an impression of unity, strength and confidence. Nor, as Lloyd George's 'Land Campaign' and the Buget of 1914 showed, had the fires of radical passion completely died down (**72**). Asquith himself, however, though as imperturbable as ever, was now sixty-two and set in his ways. He was soon to face the greatest challenge of his career.

2 The Impact of War

The end of the Liberal government

For a variety of reasons problems of defence and foreign policy were relatively subsidiary issues before the summer of 1914. But the outbreak of war on the Continent in late July and Germany's ultimatum to Belgium on 2 August immediately brought these questions to the forefront of public attention, and presented Asquith's Cabinet with its 'moment of truth'. Should Great Britain intervene in the war? And if so, would the Liberal government and party unite behind this policy (51)? As Asquith wrote to his confidante, Venetia Stanley, on the day of the ultimatum: 'I suppose a good ¾ of our own party in the House of Commons are for absolute non-interference at any price. It will be a shocking thing if at such a moment we break up – with no one to take our place' (32).

The divisions within the Cabinet over these vital problems and the reasons for them, were both less clearcut and more complex than previously imagined, as Cameron Hazlehurst has shown (32). As between the 'interventionists' on the one hand (Grey, Asquith, Churchill), conscious of the 'debt of honour' we owed to France as a result of the (secret) agreements already entered into, and concerned even more with the traditional British policy of maintaining the balance of power, and the hardline neutralists (Burns and Morley) on the other, there was also a group of 'waverers', whose leading figure was Lloyd George. The fate of the Cabinet turned in effect on his decision. In his attitude towards naval and foreign policy questions during the earlier period of Asquith's administration, Lloyd George had certainly been identified with the neutralists. But he was not an orthodox radical on these issues, and after 1911 – symbolised perhaps by his famous rebuke to Germany in his Mansion House speech during the Agadir Crisis – he adopted a tougher anti-German line and moved in his own mind nearer to the position represented by Grey and Asquith (68). Hence conviction, self-interest (resignation would destroy his political career) and Asquith's delicate tact in allowing for his refractory conscience, made it almost a foregone conclusion that Lloyd George would not end up in the neutralist camp. Grey's muddled but moving appeal in the House of Commons on the afternoon of 3 August in support, implicitly, of intervention on the side of France, together with the German invasion of Belgium, gave Lloyd George (like the other waverers in the government, and the parliamentary party) sound moral reasons for supporting a British declaration of war on Germany, which came at 11 p.m. on the night of 4 August. In the end only Morley and Burns, together with an Under-Secretary, C. P. Trevelyan, actually resigned from the government, and the mass of the country was united behind the decision for war. This outcome was in its way another political triumph for Asquith. It was, alas, to be his last.

Asquith's attitudes as leader of a nation at war were not very different from those he had assumed in time of peace: the war was just another, albeit larger, 'crisis', to be handled in the well-tried ways. 'Tell me, Mr Asquith,' someone is supposed to have asked him, 'do you take an interest in the war?' As Prime Minister he believed his role was only a 'supervisory and coordinating' one: the running of the war was to be left to the military and naval experts (**30**). This attitude was exemplified by the immediate appointment of Lord Kitchener — 'the Great Poster' as Margot Asquith called him — as Secretary for War (**3**).

Kitchener, the victor of Omdurman and Khartoum, was undoubtedly a popular hero, but he soon proved to be a hopeless Cabinet member. Secretive, inarticulate, suspicious, bewildered by and ignorant of politics and departmental administration, he soon aroused the contempt and hostility of most of the politicians, despite Asquith's deference to him. As a recruiting agent he was, however, superb. He envisaged a long war and appealed for half a million volunteers, who were obtained with astonishing speed in an outburst of patriotic fervour. While the drill sergeants got to work training this new mass army, the original British Expeditionary Force of five divisions, which had been sent to France under the command of Sir John French, was all but wiped out following the retreat from Mons and the battle of Ypres. By the winter of 1914–15 the combatants in France had dug themselves in and settled down to a bloody war of attrition on the Western Front.

The outbreak of war had a disruptive and demoralising effect on the Parliamentary Liberal Party. Two sections at least knew where they stood. On the left of the party a small group of doctrinaire neutralists — a mixture of pacifists, radicals and isolationists — saw their criticisms of pre-war policies confirmed, and remained throughout the war opponents of the government. Many of their leaders became associated with the Union of Democratic Control, and, like Ponsonby and Trevelyan, later ended up in the Labour party (**14**). On the opposite side of the party spectrum were an equally small group of 'hawks', mainly wealthy businessmen like Mond, Dalziel and Guest, but including also a number of radical realists like Addison, who reacted against the weak leadership of Asquith and demanded an all-out war effort, even if it meant greater coercion and controls. These were the men who formed the nucleus of the pro-Lloyd George element within the party, and who were to come into their own after December 1916. For the moment, however, the two groups cancelled one another out.

In the middle, unhappy and bewildered, stood the majority of Liberal MPs, many of them nonconformists who had only supported the government's decision for intervention reluctantly and at the last moment. That a Liberal government should have taken the country into a great war was bad enough in itself but the consequences of that fateful decision – the Defence of the Realm Act, press censorship, restrictions on aliens – seemed to threaten the Liberal ideals they held dear. Though they supported the war, they hoped it would be fought on Liberal principles, without the government dirtying its hands too much or offending the tender consciences of the Liberal rank-and-file. Their pessimism was increased by the suspension for the duration of the Welsh Church Disestablishment and Irish Home Rule Acts, and the virtual collapse of the party's organisation in the country with the resignation of Sir Robert Hudson, the outstanding secretary of the National Liberal Federation (**69**). The position of the parliamentary party was worsened too by Asquith's appointment of John Gulland to succeed the popular and effective Percy Illingworth as Chief Whip. Gulland proved incapable of either raising the morale of the Liberal backbenchers in the House of Commons, or establishing any real rapport between them and the Prime Minister, at a time when inevitably the power and status of the legislature was rapidly declining at the expense of the executive.

If the Liberal backbenchers had their grievances, so too did the Conservatives. At the outbreak of war the leaders of the English political parties, Liberal, Labour, and Conservative, agreed on an electoral truce, technically to cover by-elections but not a future general election. It also implied crying halt to the bitter domestic feuds which had divided government and opposition before the outbreak of hostilities. As the Prime Minister informed the House of Commons, government business would be confined 'to necessary matters and would not be of a controversial nature' (**52**). In effect, therefore, Asquith and Bonar Law were in collusion to stifle party hostility in the House by preventing the emergence of divisive issues, in an effort to impose unity upon their backbenchers in support of the war and the Liberal government (**97**). This served at one and the same time their patriotic and their party interests, especially since Bonar Law's position as Conservative leader was by no means secure and his party ranks (with the absence of so many Conservative MPs on war service) were sorely depleted (**52**).

This was not a strategy which appealed to many right-wing Conservatives in the House of Commons. They had long memories and, given the strong 'neutralist' tradition within the Liberal party, were sceptical of either the will or capacity of Liberal ministers to run a great war, a judgement which seemed confirmed by military events in France. They believed too that they were double-crossed by Asquith when he announced in September that both the Welsh and Irish Bills *would* be placed on the statute book. Conservative backbench frustration came out in demands for tougher actions by the government in support of the war effort, and smear campaigns against individual ministers, notably Haldane, the Lord Chancellor, who was denounced for pro-German sympathies. In all this they were spurred on and encouraged by the formidable power of the Northcliffe Press, through *The Times* and the *Daily Mail*. Within a few months of the electoral truce, party unity was a fragile thing. 'The political truce is very thin,' wrote Walter Runciman, President of the Board of Trade, to a friend in February 1915. 'If things go wrong we shall be flayed' (**105**).

Inevitably, the discontents of the backbenchers in all parts of the House appeared to be directed, whether in sorrow or in anger, against the Prime Minister. And the early months of 1915, with a continuance of the stalemate on the Western Front and no victory in sight, brought no relief to Asquith. What was wanted, wrote Lloyd George on New Year's Day 1915, was 'a clear definite victory . . . [which] will alone satisfy the public that tangible results are being achieved by the great sacrifices they are making' (**105**). But how was this to be achieved? The War Council set up in November (which included Balfour, representing the Conservatives) proved to be a clumsy and ineffective body, merely duplicating the inefficiencies of the Cabinet itself. As Hankey, its Secretary, pointed out some months later, there was 'literally no one in this country who knows or has access to, all the information, naval, military, and political, on which future plans must be based' (**74**).

It was this that helped to make the Dardanelles Campaign against Turkey in the spring of 1915 a military and naval disaster. The campaign was marred almost from the start by poor intelligence and planning, lack of cooperation between army and navy, and continual bickering between Churchill, First Lord of the Admiralty, and the aged and eccentric First Sea Lord, Admiral Fisher. After the failure of the original naval onslaught through the Straits, Fisher soon became disillusioned with the whole scheme. On 15 May, abruptly, he resigned. Only the previous day Colonel Repington had published his famous despatch in *The Times* blaming the government for the shell shortage on the Western Front, and denouncing the feebleness of its munitions policy. This was the culmination of a campaign which had been waged by the Conservative press for some weeks, and their allegations had been specifically denied by Asquith (on information from Kitchener) in a public speech on 20 April. The 'shell scandal' and Fisher's resignation precipitated a political crisis which within a few days led to the establishment of a Coalition government, and thus the demise of England's 'last Liberal Government' (**77**). Why did this come about?

A number of historians, following Lord Beaverbrook, have emphasised the primary importance of the Fisher resignation in initiating the crisis, because this gave Bonar Law a clear-cut issue on which he could present Asquith with an ultimatum and demand a reconstruction of his government (**17**). Asquith acquiesced in order to prevent a parliamentary debate which would have exposed his own and his government's deficiencies. He saved his own skin, but only at the price of yielding to the Conservatives. The inauguration of the Coalition represents, therefore, 'a triumph in party warfare of the Conservatives' (**94**). This is far too simple a view. As Professor Wilson has himself shown, the 'shell scandal' was as important if not more important in producing the 'May Crisis' than Lord Fisher's resignation; and the attack on the government had already begun two days before the latter's resignation, when a group of Tory backbenchers threatened a parliamentary debate on the munitions issue. It was they, not the members of the Conservative front bench, who began the 'Tory Revolt'. Bonar Law's 'ultimatum' to Asquith was in fact not an attempt to destroy his government but to sustain it, and the Conservative leader hoped that by avoiding an open confrontation between his rebels and the ministry, he would retain party and national unity, and his own leadership. Professor W. A. S. Hewins, the leader of the Tory rebels, hit the nail on the head when he wrote in his diary on 18 May: 'The Liberal newspapers attribute this action to the Opposition *leaders* though some deny that Bonar Law forced on the change of government. . . . Our experience of course is that B. L. and Co. have always up to the last moment deprecated and discouraged strong action' (**105**).

In fact, Bonar Law's letter of 17 May was in no sense an ultimatum nor a demand for an outright coalition; and was only sent *after* he had discussed the political crisis that morning with Lloyd George and Asquith [**doc. 2a**]. The initiative for a coalition seems to have come from Lloyd George and, as he tells us in his *War Memoirs*, it was agreed to by the three leaders 'in less than a quarter of an hour' (**8**). Hence Bonar Law's letter was really a 'put-up job' to enable him to obtain the agreement of his colleagues to arrangements which had already been concocted; and their consent was quickly if reluctantly given. 'If our help is asked by the government,' wrote Austen Chamberlain to his chief that evening, 'we *must* give it. God knows each of us would willingly avoid this fearful responsibility . . . ' (**89**). The Prime Minister's invitation to the Conservative leader to participate in a new Coalition government was therefore in a sense *his* ultimatum; and the responsibility for the formation of the Coalition lies as much if not more with Asquith than Bonar Law. What were his motives?

There were of course (as in the not dissimilar situation of 1940) sound general arguments in 1915 for a coalition; and Asquith suggested later that he had 'come, with increasing conviction, to the conclusion that the continued prosecution of the war requires what is called a "broad-based" Government' (**2**). On Wednesday 12 May, however, he said in reply to a parliamentary question that no coalition was contemplated: on the following Monday the new Coalition government was a *fait accompli*. This uncharacteristic speed of decision, carried through without consulting his party and surprising even his politically acute wife, implied some compelling reason for change. It was not fears of a public debate in parliament that worried Asquith, particularly on the Fisher issue, since it would be difficult for the opposition to defend the Admiral's quixotic behaviour, and (thanks to the absence of many Conservative MPs on war service) the Liberals now had a reasonable majority in the House. What alarmed Asquith, as has been argued convincingly by M. D. Pugh (**89**), was the prospect of facing a forthcoming general election. This was due, under the Parliament Act, either at the end of 1915 or at the latest in the following January. Even if an attempt was made by Parliament to pass a special Bill prolonging its own life, this would be subject to the veto of the House of Lords which could thus precipitate an election – an election which Asquith believed the divided and unsuccessful Liberals were bound to lose.

Coalition provided a possible escape route. Speed and secrecy were essential to his plan in order to save the Liberals from themselves, since they were bound to oppose any suggestion of a coalition. The mid-May crises were therefore the occasion rather than the cause of Asquith's decision. Inviting the Conservatives into the government was a way in which he could preserve himself, his party, and national unity; and, as we have seen, Bonar Law's motives were not dissimilar. Timidity and a dogged patriotism meant that he too contemplated a general election in wartime with abhorrence; even if the Conservatives won, he said, 'nothing could have prevented that . . . being held on ordinary party lines . . . with effects most disastrous to the country' (**89**). Hence the formation of the new government represented 'a coalition of the front benches against the back' (**54**).

Even in the distribution of offices the formation of the Coalition on 19 May hardly represents a victory for the Conservatives. Bonar Law went to the Colonial Office, Austen Chamberlain to the India Office, and Balfour was made First Lord of the Admiralty. Five other leading Conservatives, including Carson, Curzon and Long, were given minor Cabinet posts; and Arthur Henderson was brought into the government to represent Labour. The key offices were still retained by Liberals: but Liberals who were either pro-Asquith or had strong support within the party. Grey continued as Foreign Secretary, Crewe became Lord President, McKenna replaced Lloyd George at the Exchequer and the latter became head of the new Ministry of Munitions; Runciman continued at the Board of Trade. The two sacrificial Liberal lambs were Haldane and Churchill: the former was both unpopular and easily expendable, and the latter was not only damned for the failure of his Dardanelles project, but involved (so it was rumoured) in intrigues in connection with the Repington despatch. He was shunted off to the ignominy of the Duchy of Lancaster (**99**, III).

In many ways Asquith's cabinet-making was a brilliant piece of political *legerdemain*. His own political supremacy was apparently maintained; the Conservatives (except for Balfour who offered no personal challenge) were kept out of the actual running of the war; and the key economic posts were retained by Liberal Free Traders. But there were obvious weaknesses in the new structure. Kitchener survived as Secretary for War, despite the fact that he was the butt of the Northcliffe Press and his removal had been regarded as a major reason for the establishment of the Coalition. He was still undoubtedly popular with the public; and from Asquith's point of view the Field Marshal remained a splendid 'political umbrella' beneath which to shelter from the storms of opposition criticism. Then the Conservative backbenchers had their misgivings, since their leaders had entered the new government without conditions when it was increasingly clear that the Asquithian system of waging war was almost discredited. The Liberal backbenchers and junior ministers (many of whom had lost their jobs in the reshuffle) were even more shocked and outraged [**doc. 3a**]. Asquith was forced to justify his actions before a meeting of the Parliamentary Liberal Party on 19 May, where in a typically defensive but emotional speech he was able to win over his critics amid general acclamation [**doc. 3b**]. This success gave Asquith perhaps an over-sanguine view of his strength as Prime Minister. His new government had obtained the grudging support of Parliament and the country, which was willing at least to give it a chance to prove itself. But in the end its survival would depend on its ability to win the war.

From Asquith to Lloyd George

The advent of the Coalition did little to stiffen Asquith's resolve, or to produce any radical change in either the direction or the course of the war. The dismal tale of defeat and stalemate continued. The one great success of the new government was Lloyd George's work at the Ministry of Munitions. There his energy, confidence and dynamism infused a new spirit into war production. The ministry was run like an up-to-date business concern. 'Men of push and go' were brought in from outside to get things moving, and Lloyd George himself dealt ruthlessly with the problems of labour, red tape and inefficiency that impeded the output of munitions. Within a year the task had been virtually completed. As the *Official History* stated: 'He laid the foundations of the Ministry's productive capacity on a scale so vast that it was almost sufficient . . . to carry the country to the end of the war' (**78**).

The successes of Lloyd George at the production level made him increasingly critical of Asquith's dilatory and timorous methods at the centre. The Prime Minister's inability to deal with Kitchener or to stand up to the generals; his failure to set up an effective War Committee; his reliance on orthodox men and orthodox measures; his lack of fire and imagination – all this made Lloyd George more and more pessimistic about the outcome of the War. 'Too late in moving here! Too late in moving there! . . . In this war the footsteps of the Allied forces have been dogged by the mocking spectre of "Too late"!' (**108**): that was his judgement on his own government in a speech in the House of Commons in December 1915. These sentiments were shared by others, both inside and outside the government. Churchill soon chafed at his subordinate position at the Duchy of Lancaster and went off to command a battalion in France (**99**, III). Carson also resigned in disgust at Asquith's pusillanimity, and became the leading backbench Conservative critic of the government, supported by men like Milner in the House of Lords and, of course, the Northcliffe Press. The main bone of contention between Asquith and his critics soon became the issue of conscription. Conscription symbolised for its supporters an approach to the war based on the compulsory mobilisation of all the resources needed to win, that seemed incompatible with the voluntarist principles of Asquith. The issues of 'freedom' and 'organisation', as Taylor has put it, were joined in combat (**54**).

Asquith, like most Liberals, was a convinced opponent of conscription. But, concerned with the problems of maintaining party unity and the clamour of his critics, he launched the 'Derby Scheme' in October 1915, named after the new Director-General of Recruiting. This was a typically Asquithian compromise. It called on all men to 'attest' their willingness to serve if called upon, and was regarded by the Prime Minister as an alternative to conscription, though (since the scheme depended on registration) it could also be regarded as a step towards it. He did suggest, however, that stronger measures would be taken if the scheme failed to produce the required number of recruits. It did fail: and Asquith came to accept the inevitability of some sort of conscription, though he strove desperately to put off the evil day. Early in 1916 he introduced a new plan for the compulsory call-up of unmarried men between eighteen and forty-one. But this scheme was eventually swept aside by the House of Commons in May (partly as a result of the panic induced by the Easter Rising) and another Act was passed introducing universal military service. Asquith accepted this, largely to prevent the break-up of his Cabinet; Sir John Simon, the Home Secretary, had already resigned in January over the earlier milder Act. But the Prime Minister's belated conversion to conscription did him little good with his enemies – or with his friends. As Hankey commented: 'The fact was that the people who want compulsory service don't want Asquith, while those who want Asquith don't want compulsory service; so he fell between two stools' (**109**).

Asquith's lack of moral courage and his purely political approach to the conscription question, particularly upset his fellow Liberals. 'In his own party', wrote a leading Liberal journalist, 'all is chilled and changed' (**13**). For old-fashioned Liberals who had already been forced to swallow McKenna's protectionist duties, the acceptance of conscription was another nail in the coffin of traditional Liberalism, which merely confirmed their impotence and disillusion. For them, as for Asquith, it marked something of a turning point. 'Asquith's wartime premiership reached its climax in May 1916 . . . all that followed was the *dénouement*' (**105**).

The triumph of conscription did little in fact to placate the critics of Asquith, notably Lloyd George. It was the latter's threats of resignation that had helped to push the Prime Minister towards his formal acceptance of universal military service; but this did nothing to transform immediately the anomalous political position of the Minister of Munitions. In many ways Lloyd George's belligerence in speech and action and his pro-conscription stance, increased his isolation within the Liberal party. Nor did it do much either in removing the suspicions that most orthodox Conservatives held of him as a selfish power-seeker: hence his friendship with Conservative outsiders like Carson, and newspapermen like Lord Riddell. For these reasons, and because he still had a healthy respect for the political skill of Asquith and his command of Liberal support, he was not yet prepared to challenge him directly, even though the spring of 1916 saw a further deterioration in the Allied military position. By June Lloyd George was once again pessimistic and near resignation. In that month, however, his political position was suddenly transformed by the drowning of Kitchener en route for Russia. Despite the fact that he had recently written to Asquith asserting that 'I am completely out of sympathy with the spirit and method of the war direction', he took over the War Office the following month, believing that through it he could control the generals – especially the CIGS, Sir William Robertson – and remodel the British war effort (**78**). In this he was soon disillusioned. Robertson proved to be both wilier and more stubborn than he had anticipated. Increasing frustration led to a growing resolve, reinforced by the catastrophe of the Somme that summer, that somehow the direction of the war must be changed.

In mid-November, while attending an Allied Conference in Paris with Asquith, Lloyd George revealed his thoughts to Hankey who was accompanying them. Hankey persuaded him to abandon the idea of resignation, and suggested the formation of a small War Committee, independent of the Cabinet, to be headed by 'a man of unimpaired energy and great driving power'. Since Lloyd George had been thinking along similar lines and regarded himself as just such a man, he was determined to get the plan accepted by Asquith. To achieve this he needed the support of Bonar Law as Conservative leader; and, as it turned out, once again (as in 1915) obscure events within the Parliamentary Conservative party produced just the leverage needed to overcome Bonar Law's suspicions and push the two men together. On 8 November, on a minor issue relating to the sale of confiscated enemy property in Nigeria, Sir Edward Carson led sixty-four Conservatives into the opposition lobby – only seventy-one voted with their leader! This was a clear attack on Bonar Law for sustaining Asquith's war policy; but the real target was the government itself.

The results of the Nigerian vote showed that Lloyd George had an obvious ally in Carson in pushing his plans for a new War Committee, and that Bonar Law, if he wished to retain his own leadership and avoid a Tory split, would have to support some such plan for reinvigorating the direction of the war. As Beaverbrook observes: 'The way of salvation, if it could be taken, was a combination of the three men – Lloyd George, Bonar Law and Carson – which would save Bonar Law's position, maintain the unity of the Tory party . . . restore the national fortunes, and lead to the vigorous prosecution of the war . . .' (**17**, II).

It was Beaverbrook who, with these aims in mind, helped to bring his friend, Bonar Law, into touch with the two other collaborators in a series of meetings arranged in late November. It was eventually agreed by the so-called Triumvirate that, while Asquith should continue as Prime Minister, a small Committee would be set up under the chairmanship of Lloyd George to deal with the actual running of the war. The first approach to Asquith on these lines by Bonar Law on 25 November, was rejected firmly but politely [**doc. 4a**]; and both sides then drew back to organise support and reconsider their positions. On Friday 1 December, Lloyd George threw down the gauntlet to Asquith by threatening resignation unless his definite proposals for a new War Committee were accepted. Asquith again demurred, insisting that 'whatever changes are made in the composition or function of the War Committee, the Prime Minister must be its Chairman'. It was this clash of wills that led to the political crisis of the first week of December 1916 [**doc. 4d**].

On the following day Lloyd George, knowing that the Conservative ministers were to meet on Sunday, sent his laconic note to Bonar Law: 'The life of the country depends on resolute action by you now.' At the meeting the ministers passed an equivocal vote of 'no confidence' in Asquith, while remaining critical of Lloyd George; adopting in fact a muddled posture of 'neutrality' as between the two men. But it was enough to force Asquith to reopen negotiations with Lloyd George and Bonar Law, and in effect accept their terms. As Lloyd George wrote in his *War Memoirs*: 'At the interview which ensued Mr Asquith and I discussed the whole situation in the friendliest spirit and ultimately came to a complete understanding' (**8**, I). Yet by the following morning that understanding had been shattered to pieces. This was due, ostensibly at least, to the publication that Monday of the notorious article in *The Times* denigrating Asquith, and, in relation to the membership of any new War Committee, arguing that he was 'unfit to be fully charged with the supreme direction of the war' (**105**). Asquith concluded that the article had been inspired by Lloyd George; and, despite the latter's denial of the charge, he repudiated the agreement made on the previous day [**doc. 4b**]. The Prime Minister then consulted with his leading Liberal colleagues and, spurred on by their support and confident that he would obtain the backing of the leading Conservative ministers save Bonar Law, decided to accept the consequences of the break with Lloyd George. The following day Lloyd George resigned [**doc. 4c**]: but instead of supporting Asquith, the Conservative ministers followed their leader, Bonar Law, out of office, and with the collapse of his government Asquith himself resigned that evening.

It has been argued by Beaverbrook (followed by his loyal disciple, A. J. P. Taylor) that Asquith's resignation was merely a tactical device to humiliate Lloyd George by revealing his inability to form a government, a failure which would then be followed by the triumphant re-installation of the former Prime Minister (**17, 53**). In the light of Asquith's mental and emotional state on the Monday, when the will to go on seemed suddenly to have deserted him, this seems extremely unlikely. In any case it was not to be. Bonar Law made the gesture of trying to form a government, and then handed the problem over to Lloyd George. Lloyd George was able to secure the support of the Conservatives, Labour, and about 100 Liberal MPs, just under half of the Parliamentary Party. 'In the afternoon', Frances Stevenson, Lloyd George's secretary, wrote in her diary on 7 December, 'D. was in high spirits. "I think I shall be Prime Minister before 7 o'clock", he said to me. And he was' (**11**).

What brought Lloyd George to power? Many contemporaries believed that he was intriguing with the Conservatives to oust Asquith and replace him as Prime Minister virtually from the beginning of the first Coalition – if not before [**doc. 2b**]; and this view has been endorsed by Professor Trevor Wilson in his brilliant study of *The Downfall of the Liberal Party*. Other historians, however, have adopted a more generous view of Lloyd George's conduct (**75**). For, while it would be absurd to deny that Lloyd George wished to become Prime Minister – a not ignoble ambition for a politician of genius – the evidence that he actively 'conspired' to achieve this during the latter months of 1916 is rather thin. Indeed, it has been argued that: 'paradoxically Lloyd George achieved the office of Prime Minister . . . at a time when he did not want it or expect to secure it' (**78**).

The 'conspiracy' theory becomes rather shaky when one remembers that Asquith was kept fully informed of the plans of the Triumvirate from 20 November onwards, both personally and by letter. Moreover, as Bonar Law insisted and as Carson and Lloyd George agreed, the basis of their agreement was that Asquith should continue as Prime Minister. Lloyd George neither wished for nor believed he had the political power to achieve the overthrow of Asquith: provided that the direction of the war could be made more effective – and that the proposed War Committee under his chairmanship would accomplish – he was content (**108**). What changed the situation dramatically was Asquith's repudiation on Monday 6 December, in a provocative manner, of the agreement he had made the previous day with Lloyd George, followed later by his own resignation. While Lloyd George then offered to serve under either Bonar Law or Balfour, Asquith indignantly refused to accept any subordinate place. It was only after these events that political opinion swung towards Lloyd George without his going out actively to seek it: 'the King's Government must be carried on'. It was Asquith who, wittingly or unwittingly, created the circumstances which brought Lloyd George to power. 'At one moment', writes Lord Beaverbrook, 'Asquith was everything; in the next he was nothing. The great illusion of indispensability vanished in a night' (**17**, II).

The domination of Lloyd George, 1916–18

Lloyd George's ability to form a government was based ultimately on the support of a bloc of some 120 Liberal MPs, and their support had been forthcoming at the crucial moment as a result of the assiduous canvassing of the Prime Minister's henchman, Christopher Addison. But though Lloyd George could rely on a clear majority in the House of Commons, the problems of cabinet-making were particularly difficult, owing to the refusal of Asquith and all the Liberal ex-ministers to serve in the new government. In the end, therefore, Lloyd George was forced to rely almost entirely on the Conservatives to provide the mainstay of his ministry; his new War Cabinet consisted of himself, Bonar Law, Milner, Curzon, and Arthur Henderson representing Labour. The only Liberals who agreed to serve in the government were those of the second rank, such as Addison, and a man like Herbert Fisher, who was brought in from academic life to head the Board of Education. The appointment of Churchill, one of the few ex-Liberal ministers whom Lloyd George really wanted, was vetoed by the Conservatives. The country was therefore faced with the extraordinary spectacle of a Liberal Prime Minister whose government was made up mainly of Conservatives, supported in the House of Commons by one section of Liberals; while the leader of the party, supported by the majority of the Liberals, sat on the opposition benches.

The events of December 1916 seemed, therefore, at the very least, to have delivered a powerful body-blow at the unity of the Liberal party. As Liberal leader Asquith controlled the party machine – head-quarters, funds and officials – and had the backing of the National Liberal Federation; and John Gulland continued as Chief Whip. Lloyd George on his side appointed his own Coalition Liberal Chief Whip, Captain 'Freddie' Guest (after a brief tenure by Neil Primrose). Later he began to build up his own party fund through the sale of offices. He also acquired the *Daily Chronicle* as a rival to the generally pro-Asquithian Liberal press. Yet neither side was prepared to push its differences too far. Both sets of Whips canvassed all Liberal MPs, a sensible provision in fact since the Parliamentary Liberal Party was not divided into two clear-cut pro- and anti-government groups, as the considerable number of abstentions in important debates reveals. In the constituencies too, though there was Asquithian pressure to ensure that the candidates of their persuasion were selected to stand at by-elections (as at Derby in late December) there was no attempt by either side to put forward rival candidates. The party truce was thus maintained; and despite the underlying bitterness and antagonism between the two sections, the formal unity of the Liberal party remained until the end of the war.

Moreover, the self-effacing attitude of Asquith towards the government tended to undermine the credibility and effectiveness of his supporters as a real opposition. For, having refused to serve in the government on the disingenuous grounds that he could give it 'more effective support from outside', Asquith conceived it to be his duty to adopt a pose of 'sober and responsible opposition' (2). This meant doing nothing to imperil national unity by attacking the government wholeheartedly or voting against it, even on issues which clearly affronted the Liberal conscience. Asquith was further inhibited by his reluctance to appear motivated by personal animus against Lloyd George, and the need to show that the opposition was no less patriotic than the government. 'Asquith's predicament' after December 1916 was, therefore, as Barry McGill has written, 'how to use his political prestige and his power as a party leader, to support the war effort without identifying himself and his followers with the government' (79).

Those followers were impaled, even more uncomfortably, on the horns of the same dilemma: were they or were they not opponents of the government? This was a question to which they were unable to give a clear and logical answer; and their confusion was the more confounded by their own internal divisions over key questions, such as the relationship between Lloyd George and the generals and the Lansdowne peace proposals. Most of them were prepared in principle (in the words of one Liberal Federation resolution) 'to give support to the king's government engaged in the effective prosection of the war' (**94**). But they were not prepared to accept the tame attitude adopted by their leader towards individual government measures, especially as the Liberal opposition now embraced not only loyal Asquithians, but the much more radical anti-government group of 1914. Hence Liberal backbenchers like J. M. Hogge, William Pringle and Leif Jones, were prepared to denounce the government with vigour day in and day out, even though the Liberal front bench remained aloof.

Despite the public amity of Asquith and Lloyd George, their personal antagonism increased rather than diminished. This was seen in Asquith's bitter rejection of the proposal, conveyed to him by Lord Reading in the spring of 1917, that he should join the government. 'Under no conditions', wrote Asquith, 'wd. I serve in a Govt. of wh. Ll. G. was the head. I had learned by long and close association to mistrust him profoundly. I knew him to be incapable of loyalty or lasting gratitude . . .' (**94**). This attitude (so different from Asquith's 'statesmanlike' reasons for rejecting office in December 1916) was symptomatic of the hardening of the ranks on both sides of the Liberal party that occurred in the later months of 1917. And what divided the supporters of Lloyd George from those of Asquith, was not so much their origins and background, but rather (as had always been the case) the answer they gave to the question: how should the war be fought, and under which leader? (**67**)

The increasing division between the two sides was seen in a series of bitter debates in the House of Commons on the Indian Cotton Duties, the Representation of the People Bill, and Irish conscription. These debates clearly revealed the profound hostility of many members of the Liberal opposition (and other sections of the House) to various aspects of government policy; though they showed equally the growing crystallisation of a belligerently pro-Lloyd George party. Forty-nine Liberals voted against the Cotton Duties Bill, and fifty-nine supported it. Over the Franchise Bill, Liberals were so outraged by the right-wing proposals to retain plural voting and disenfranchise conscientious objectors, that the moderate Asquithian, Herbert Samuel, was able to lead 106 Liberals into the opposition lobby. On none of these issues could Asquith bring himself to vote against the government: he failed even to oppose Irish conscription in April 1918, which led to mass abstention by his followers on the Second Reading of the Military Ser-

vice Bill which contained the proposal, followed by its practical aban-
donment by Lloyd George. Hence the actions of the Liberal opposition
in these debates indicates almost as much frustration and irritation
with Asquith, as with the government. 'Asquith decided to occupy a
political no-man's-land; where he was neither quite attacking nor quite
supporting the Prime Minister. . . . As the price of avoiding a
severance between the two sections of Liberals, Asquith doomed his
party to impotence' (**94**).

This was true also of the 'Maurice Debate' in May 1918 – the most
famous occasion during Lloyd George's wartime ministry when the
opposition divided against the government. The debate arose out of
the assertion by Major-General Sir Frederick Maurice that the figures
given by the Prime Minister of the number of troops in France at the
beginning of the year, were false. Asquith thereupon introduced a motion demanding the establishment of a Commons Select Committee to
investigate the charges, a demand which Lloyd George treated as a
vote of confidence. The subsequent debate was important, not because
it was an isolated example of Liberals dividing against the government
since, as we have seen, clearly it was not; but because it was the only occasion when Asquith led and voted with the opposition. Even so, he insisted in his speech that he was not trying to defeat the government,
and his performance was a feeble one. Lloyd George easily triumphed
with a vote for the government of 298 against 106; 98 Liberals supported Asquith, and 72 Lloyd George. Even though many Liberals
abstained, the figures show starkly the clear division among Liberal
backbenchers between two rival conceptions of war policy and war
leadership; a division which is reinforced by the high correlation between the opposition's voting on this issue and the contentious ones
that had preceded it (**67**).

The 'Maurice Debate' also highlighted Lloyd George's virtually
unassailable political ascendancy, and his growing domination of the
machinery of war and government (**83**). It showed unmistakably that
the opposition could neither turn out the government, nor propound
any practical alternatives to the policies of the Prime Minister. The
government itself had been strengthened and its Liberal complexion
emphasised by the appointment in July 1917 of the Asquithian
renegade, Ewen Montagu, to the India Office, and Churchill to the
Ministry of Munitions. In the same year, Lloyd George was able to impose his views on the Admiralty through the adoption of the convoy
system and the dismissal of Jellicoe as First Sea Lord; and even to assert
more forceful control over the generals, symbolised by the sacking of
Robertson in February 1918, though Haig remained (**18**). As the tide

of war suddenly moved in favour of the Allies after July 1918, so, inevitably, it was Lloyd George and his supporters who reaped the political rewards in terms of public acclaim. The Asquithian Liberals became more and more an irrelevant, unimportant and despairing minority.

Shortly after the Maurice Debate the minds of Lloyd George and his Liberal confidants began to turn towards the prospect of a general election. There were sound reasons for this. The last election had been held in December 1910, and the existing House of Commons was now hopelessly out-of-date as a representative assembly. The situation became even more anomalous after the passing of the Representation of the People Act in February 1918, which revolutionised the British political system by trebling the electorate and introducing a radical redistribution of seats. Moreover, a successful election would give Lloyd George a clear mandate for fighting the war to a finish, thus scotching any possibility of a negotiated peace and revealing even more clearly the futility of the opposition. The problem that faced him, however, was that he remained 'a Prime Minister without a party' (**84**). He was obviously not a Conservative; but neither did he control any part of the official machinery of the Liberal party, which was firmly in Asquithian hands. This meant that in the event of a general election, his Liberal supporters would be wide open to attack.

The situation was tackled after the Maurice Debate when steps were taken to set up a tenuous 'Coalition Liberal' organisation under Guest as Chief Whip, to bargain with the Conservatives for what they could get. By July, well before the end of hostilities, a committee of Coalition Liberals had produced plans for fighting the general election in collaboration with the Conservatives, and these were endorsed by Lloyd George [**doc. 5**]. The suggested proposals were carried out in the course of the next few months, and by the end of October Guest was able to report to his Chief: 'I have come to an agreement with Mr Bonar Law that we should receive their support, where necessary, for 150 Lloyd George candidates' (**94**). This was the origin of the notorious 'coupon' (as it was dubbed by Asquith), or official letter of government endorsement, signed by Lloyd George and Bonar Law and sent to all electoral candidates who were deemed to be coalition supporters. It was on this basis that Lloyd George fought the 'coupon election' in December 1918, as soon as possible after the signing of the Armistice. He was opposed by the Asquithian Liberals – often in a half-hearted fashion – and, more vigorously, by the Labour party, which had formally withdrawn from the Coalition on 15 November.

Why did Lloyd George fight the election in collaboration with the

Conservatives, and thus inevitably doom the Liberals to further protracted division? Originally, as we have seen, he thought in terms of a wartime election in which he would head a national coalition committed solely to victory. But once an electoral alliance had been concluded with the Conservatives in July, it was tempting to use it to establish a new peacetime coalition based on the continuance of his own personal supremacy and national unity, accompanied by a programme of post-war reform and reconstruction. It is true that the use of the 'coupon' involved Lloyd George in waging political war on the majority of his fellow-Liberals – he still considered himself to be one. But this, he could argue, was their own fault for having consistently opposed his wartime government, characterised by Asquith yet again refusing a government post (that of Lord Chancellor) in November 1918. Asquith's attitude seemed to indicate only too well the difficulties that would face Lloyd George in adopting the other possible alternative: a break with the Conservatives and reunion with the Asquithian Liberals. Even apart from the delicate personal problem of the leadership, why should he tie himself to an apparently out-of-date and discredited party, with no guarantee of electoral victory? In the jingoistic atmosphere of 1918, a *mariage de convenance* with the Conservatives meant almost certain success, and therefore the opportunity to use his enormous abilities and prestige in a constructive way to deal with the problems of the post-war world. (**113**). Furthermore, Lloyd George could point out, not unreasonably, that at a time when everything favoured the Conservatives as the 'patriotic' party, he had at least saved 159 Liberals (the final tally of 'couponed' candidates) from the possibility of defeat; and indeed 136 of these were eventually elected.

There has been much discussion among historians on how the original 150 'couponed' Liberals were chosen. As Trevor Wilson has clearly shown, there is little basis for Lloyd George's claim that the 'acid test' in deciding which Liberals were chosen was whether they voted for or against the government in the Maurice Debate; though it does seem that an important reason for proscribing some Liberals was their *general* anti-government voting record (**67**). Yet, as Wilson has also emphasised, *who* was chosen was less important in the election than *the number* chosen: all 'couponless' Liberals above the final magic figure of 159, whoever they were, were regarded as *ipso facto* anti-Coalitionists and ripe for slaughter (**93**).

And slaughtered they were. The result of the 1918 election was a massive victory for the Coalition: more than 500 supporters of the government were returned, 470 of them with the 'coupon'. The Independent Liberals numbered less than 30, and nearly all the leading Asquithians, including Asquith himself, were defeated. Even Labour, which was fighting for the first time as an independent party, did better, gaining more than 2 million votes and 63 seats. Certainly, Lloyd George's plan for plucking Liberal brands from the fire was successful in so far as 136 'couponed' Liberals were returned. But it was the 'swing to the right' that was one of the most significant trends in the election of 1918, as revealed by the nearly 400 Conservatives who crowded the benches in the House of Commons, and most of them would have been there even if the 'coupon' had never existed. The Coalition Liberals were swept into parliament on the Conservative tide, and in this inauspicious way began their brief careers as members of 'Lloyd George's Stage Army' (**87**). The Liberals were now a weak and divided force: faced on the right, by a triumphant and remorseless Conservative party, and on the left, by the independent rising power of Labour.

Part Two: Liberal Decline

3 Liberals Divided

'Coalitionists' and 'Wee Frees'

The aftermath of the 'coupon election' faced Liberals with the question which had hovered over them uneasily since 'the parting of the ways' in December 1916: were they two sections of one party, or were they two separate parties? Though some attempt was made in 1919 to maintain the fiction of one party, particularly by the coalitionist Liberal rank-and-file, the sense of bitterness and betrayal felt by the opposition Liberals, and their insistence on *independence* as the hallmark of Liberal allegiance, made a rupture between the two sides almost inevitable. By the spring of 1919, the Independent Liberals (or 'Wee Frees' as they came to be called) had set up their own separate parliamentary organisation, with Sir Donald Maclean as leader (until Asquith returned), and J. M. Hogge and G. R. Thorne as Joint Chief Whips (**69**). Lloyd George replied by establishing his own parliamentary organisation under George Lambert as Chairman. He then took the war into the enemy's camp by deliberately putting up a Coalition Liberal candidate to oppose Sir John Simon at the Spen Valley by-election in December 1919. For the first time, Liberal fought Liberal, with the result that Labour won the seat. However, two months later, in February 1920, Asquith won a notable victory in the Paisley by-election, and returned triumphantly to the House of Commons to resume the leadership of the Independent Liberals. Their reply to Spen Valley was a policy of out-and-out warfare against the Coalition Liberals, and they now declared that they would put up candidates against them in by-elections, as if they were members of another political party, even if this meant defying the wishes of a local Liberal association. The final breach came at the Leamington Liberal Conference in May 1920, when the pro-Coalitionist contingent, infuriated by the unremitting hostility of the Independent majority, marched out, leaving their opponents in effect to reassert their control over the whole Liberal party organisation outside Wales.

But though the Coalition Liberals were now beyond the pale as far as official Liberalism was concerned, they regarded themselves as

'Liberals still'; and at ministerial level Liberalism was important both in terms of personnel and policy. Seven Liberals, apart from Lloyd George himself, held office in the new, enlarged peacetime Cabinet; and it was Liberal ministers – notably Addison, Macnamara, Mond and Fisher – who were mainly responsible for the important social reforms of the period in the fields of housing, unemployment, and education (**113**). In this they were strongly supported by Edwin Montagu (himself responsible for more enlightened policies at the India Office) and indeed, in the early halcyon days at least, by the Prime Minister himself. It was these men too who fought a rearguard action, largely unsuccessful in the end, against the drastic cuts imposed on the social services by the Tory-inspired 'Geddes Axe', a policy which Lloyd George, dependent on Conservative votes, felt he had to accept (**87**).

The Coalition Liberals were very much 'a ministerial party, rather than a parliamentary one' (**87**). The exact role of the rank-and-file, damned by the Wee Frees, largely ignored by Lloyd George, and overshadowed by the vast Conservative majority, was difficult to determine. They made the ritualistic obeisances to Liberalism over questions like the 'Black and Tans', intervention in Russia and, above all, Free Trade: sixty Coalition Liberals abstained in June 1919 over a proposal to extend the McKenna duties. But these gestures were of little practical consequence, and as a parliamentary force they were bereft of either oratory or ideas. Once it became clear to Lloyd George in the course of 1919 that the way back to the one true Liberal party was blocked for his Coalitionist supporters, he worked hard for the creation of a centre party which would fuse them with the Conservatives into a powerful anti-socialist bloc. Hence his absurd attacks on the 'Bolshevism' of the Labour party. The Conservatives were not unwilling to absorb them, as they had done their Liberal Unionist predecessors in an earlier generation. But in March 1920 Lloyd George was stopped in his tracks by the unexpected opposition of most of the Coalition Liberal ministers to the idea of 'fusion', and the clear indication that the rank-and-file, still determined to maintain their Liberalism, and disturbed by the unblushing opportunism of their leader, would follow suit. In the spring of 1920 the idea of a centre party vanished for ever.

This left the Coalition Liberals inhabiting more than ever a political limbo of their own: unable to rejoin their Liberal brethren, but unwilling to merge their identity with the Conservatives. The only thing left for them to do was to accept the logic of the situation and turn themselves into a separate political party by building up their own organisation in the country. This was the work of Charles McCurdy (Guest's successor as Chief Whip) backed by subventions from the 'Lloyd

George Fund'. More than 200 Coalition Liberal associations were set up in 1921–22, together with a series of regional councils; the party also published its own journal, the *Lloyd George Liberal Magazine*. But all this provided the shadow rather than the substance of party organisation, since it soon became clear that the Coalition Liberal party lacked any solid grass roots support, or indeed any obvious *raison d'être* in the country at large (**40**). These organisational weaknesses were both a cause and a symptom of the appalling by-election record of the Coalition Liberals between 1918 and 1922. Out of twenty-five seats they fought, they lost nine, eight of them to Labour; the other seats were retained only as a result of deliberate Conservative support. Hence the distinctiveness and influence of the Liberal wing of the Coalition became increasingly attenuated, especially after the ravages of the 'Geddes Axe', and the resignation (virtually after a Tory witch-hunt) of Addison in July 1921 and Montagu nine months later. The future of the Liberal Coalitionists, including even that of their leader, now seemed to depend on the mood of the Conservatives. And the patience of many of them was wearing thin. Sir George Younger, the influential Conservative Chairman, wrote to Bonar Law as early as 1920: 'This constant loss of C[oalition] L[iberal] seats becomes serious and I see no chance of any improvement. With poor candidates and no organisation of their own, the attrition is bound to go on and the inclusion of the Downing Street staff does no good' (**87**). Why should the Conservatives (he might have said in Metternich's words) go on propping up a mouldering corpse?

If the Liberals supporting the Coalition had their problems, so too did those in opposition. The Wee Frees insisted on their independence as Liberals, but independence for what? To this question their leaders could return no very clear or convincing answer. There was some radicalism left in the Liberal party, as evinced for example at the new Liberal summer schools; but many of the outstanding pre-war Radicals like Buxton, Trevelyan, Ponsonby and Wedgwood Benn, had joined or were preparing to join the Labour party. Too often the Liberal 'old gang' merely echoed in a more muted form the harsh economic orthodoxies of the Conservative party. 'Personally,' confessed Maclean, explaining Liberal economic policy, 'I have nothing heroic to offer. I believe we will only get things adjusted naturally by . . . simple commonsense and homely wisdom . . . the only way to get back to national health is by way of economy' (**94**). Nor was Asquith, who was seventy in 1922, able or prepared to give a strong lead or a new radical direction and purpose to the Liberal party to counter the growing success of MacDonald and the Labour party [**doc. 6**]. Even so sympathetic a friend and colleague as Grey commented: 'He is using the machine of a great political brain to rearrange old ideas' (**94**).

The weaknesses at the top were reflected also in the collapse of morale and party organisation at the local level, a collapse which had been hastened by the internecine feuds within the Liberal party in the two years following the coupon election. The results were seen in the dramatic losses to Labour in local elections, particularly in the great cities, and in the advance of Labour at the expense of Liberalism in by-elections. Between 1918 and 1922 the Independent Liberals won only five seats and lost two; and they came third in fifteen out of the twenty-four by-elections where three candidates stood. 'Apart from Scotland', wrote Herbert Gladstone ominously, 'we are making no progress.' For both Coalitionist Liberals and Wee Frees the future looked grim.

The downfall of Lloyd George, 1922

By the middle of 1921, Conservative discontent with Lloyd George and the Coalition government was mounting, especially in the constituencies. Many of the Prime Minister's policies aroused disquiet: his conciliatory attitude towards Germany, his willingness to negotiate with Bolsheviks and Sinn Feiners, his sympathy with social reform and (until the 'Geddes Axe' descended) his complacency towards the financial profligacy that often seemed to accompany it. Even more alarming perhaps were his methods of government. He still tried to act as the 'War Dictator' — arrogant, domineering and independent; he ignored and seemingly despised the House of Commons, and indeed some of his own ministers (**83**). In the eyes of ordinary Conservatives, who both feared and distrusted him, he appeared unscrupulous and insincere, lacking any sound consistent political principles, or, in a troubled post-war world, a clear sense of direction and purpose. His cavalier attitude towards the 'sale of honours' and his amassing of the 'Lloyd George Fund', seemed to debase still further the standards of public life. It was for these Conservatives that Stanley Baldwin spoke when he denounced Lloyd George a year later at the Carlton Club meeting as 'a dynamic force' who might destroy the Tory party as he had destroyed the Liberals (**107**).

Three years after the Armistice the superhuman image of Lloyd George was beginning to fade. The impact of economic depression and heavy unemployment showed that there were problems that even the 'Welsh Wizard' could not solve, and quickly ended the mirage of 'a land fit for heroes to live in' (**42**). Disillusionment among the working class was accompanied also by an outburst of trade union militancy, to which the Prime Minister responded with his old mixture of threats, blandishments and delay. This time, however, it was received with resentment and hostility, especially by the miners, who regarded themselves as betrayed by Lloyd George when he rejected the recommendation of the Sankey Commission in 1919 in favour of the nationalisation of the mines. Even more important was the steady growth of the Labour party, but this was a phenomenon that Lloyd George, bred in the old rural radical tradition, seemed unable to comprehend (**14**). For many Conservatives, however, the 'menace of socialism' was the central problem of the politics of the early 1920s, and one which they were coming to feel could only be combated effectively (especially after the failure of the attempt to establish a centre party) by a strong united independent Conservative party, freed from the encumbrance of their Liberal allies (**27**). Indeed, as the popularity of the government waned, it no longer seemed necessary for Conservatives to shelter behind the name of Lloyd George or to rely on the proxy Liberal votes which he could command in order to win an election, and many of them now fought by-elections under their own colours. The Conservative victory at the famous Newport by-election on the very eve of the decisive Carlton Club meeting underlined the message.(**45**).

Yet one must not exaggerate the extent and effectiveness of Conservative opposition to Lloyd George, at least before the crises of 1922. The 'Press Barons' might now be against him; there might be grumbling in the constituencies and outraged speeches from the Diehards in the House of Commons; but nevertheless his policies – even the Irish Treaty of December 1921 – were passed by comfortable majorities. Above all, he was strongly supported by the leading Conservative ministers, Balfour, Horne, Curzon, Birkenhead, Austen Chamberlain and, until the final showdown, Bonar Law. The retirement of Bonar Law through ill-health in May 1921, however, weakened the Coalition and removed a steadying influence within the Conservative party, for his successor as party leader, Austen Chamberlain, was both maladroit in his dealings with the parliamentary party and regarded by most of its members as too much under the thumb of Lloyd George. Hence, ironically, it was Chamberlain's leadership that helped to bring about the downfall of the Coalition he so strongly supported.

Late in 1921 Lloyd George, hoping to cash in on the successful conclusion of the Irish Treaty, began to favour an immediate general election to be fought once again as a Coalition. This would have the effect of forcing the Coalition Liberals into alliance with the Conservatives, thus producing the centre party which they had earlier rejected, and giving the Prime Minister a renewed mandate; at the same time it would cut the ground from under the feet of the dissident Tories by presenting them with a *fait accompli*. It was for these reasons that the proposal was bitterly opposed by Sir George Younger, the Conservative party chairman, in a private letter to Lloyd George, and when he deliberately published his views in the press (without consulting his party leader) the effect was to bring out into the open the underlying hostility of much Conservative sentiment towards the continuance of the Coalition. Lloyd George might protest that he was 'not going to be bullied by a second-rate brewer', but in fact he postponed his election plans, while Younger remained party chairman – a revealing comment on the rapid erosion of the Prime Minister's power (**94**).

After these revelations Conservative discontent inevitably increased, especially after the failure of the Genoa Conference in the spring of 1922, and the Prime Minister's rash support for the Greeks in their conflict with Turkey that erupted a few months later. The 'Chanak Incident' in September (which could have led to war with Turkey) revealed Lloyd George's dangerously isolated position both internationally and at home. Hurriedly, the Prime Minister and Chamberlain decided on an immediate election. The latter thereupon summoned a meeting of Conservative MPs at the Carlton Club for 19 October, in order to trounce the dissidents and obtain the Conservative party's support for fighting the election as a Coalition in alliance with Lloyd George. On the face of it, there was little to stop Chamberlain: the big guns of the party were on his side, and the dissidents had no comparable leader. McCurdy, the Coalition Liberal Chief Whip, had commented to Lloyd George: 'The cardinal question is, where will our Tory friends be in a few months from now? I think the movement among the Tories for a break away from the Coalition will grow. If they find a live man to lead them it might become a stampede' (**76**). That man now appeared, at the eleventh hour, in the person of Bonar Law, whose return to active politics had been signalled by his famous rebuke to the Prime Minister over his Near Eastern policy in a letter to *The Times* on 6 October: 'We cannot act alone as the policemen of the world' (**53**).

Bonar Law's decision to attend the Carlton Club meeting and oppose Chamberlain gave the Conservative dissidents not only a respected spokesman, but also an alternative Prime Minister – a vital need if the Coalition was to be destroyed without a political vacuum being created that the Labour party could fill. The meeting rejected Chamberlain's proposal by 185 votes to 88, and decided to fight the election as an independent party. Though the speeches of Bonar Law and Baldwin doubtless had some effect, it seems clear that most MPs, representing the views of their constituency parties, had already made up their minds before the meeting to vote against the continuance of any electoral alliance with Lloyd George (**76**). Lloyd George immediately resigned, thus beginning his long sojourn in the political wilderness [**doc. 7**]. 'He was brought down, as he had been raised up, by a revolt of the backbenchers' (**92**). Bonar Law then became Prime Minister; and, since most of the ex-coalitionist Conservative ministers refused to serve, was forced to establish (in Churchill's phrase) 'a government of the second eleven'. Nevertheless, it was as leader of an independent Conservative administration that he faced the electorate in the autumn of 1922.

The general election of 1922 represented, wrote the *Nation*, 'a state of confusion unknown in any former election. The old party lines are gone' (**76**). At least four parties participated: Labour, Conservative, Liberal, and National (Lloyd George) Liberal. But who was fighting whom and over what, was difficult to determine. Hence the election depended not on policies or programmes, but 'almost entirely on atmosphere, personalities, and party image' (**98**). Moreover, the fact that so many of the electorate had not voted before, and that – as no party put up candidates in more than two-thirds of the constituencies – local issues were important and local agreements inevitable, added even further to the confusion of the contest. It was, says its historian, 'the most complex [election] of this century' (**76**).

Labour (which put up 411 candidates, its highest ever) at least was a united party, and had a programme of sorts to offer the electorate. Bonar Law too could sit back, say nothing, and rely on the growing anti-Lloyd George breeze to waft him gently back into office. The problems for the Liberals were much more serious. Lloyd George's dramatic fall from power demonstrated all too clearly his political nakedness: he had money – the 'Lloyd George Fund' – but no real party organisation to fall back on. Rejected by the Tories and detested by the Independent Liberals, his radicalism preempted by the Labour party, he was at a loss for a viable electoral strategy or an inspiring programme. He tried to adopt the old mantle of the national leader, standing between the extremes of 'revolution' and 'reaction', but the role was unconvincing, even to himself, and he soon abandoned any prospect of playing a positive part in the election. His bewildered and demoralised followers, rejecting any possibility of reunion with the Asquithians, preferred to rely on the good will of their former allies to rescue them from the *déluge*. They put up only 162 candidates, most of them in the same seats they had fought in 1918, and only seven challenged a Conservative. Nevertheless, Younger insisted firmly that there was no electoral pact with the National Liberals (only in Scotland was this defied) and about one-third of their candidates were faced with Conservative opponents. However, this still left them with more than 100 seats where the Tories (for opportunist rather than altruistic reasons) fielded no candidates, preferring to give their erstwhile allies the chance of winning the seats rather than splitting the vote and letting in Labour.

The Independent Liberals were also in an extremely difficult position. They made a determined effort to reestablish their role as a major party by putting up 328 candidates; but they found it virtually impossible to work out a clear consistent attitude to the other parties. Who was their principal enemy – Bonar Law, Lloyd George, or Ramsay MacDonald? Since they were unable to decide, their attack on each or all three of them was muffled. Without a radical programme which could challenge Labour on the left, and commanded by a leader who expected and perhaps welcomed defeat, the followers of Asquith made little impact on the British electorate.

Paradoxically, out of the confusion of the 1922 election emerged a number of clear-cut and significant results that were to shape the character of British politics for a generation. The Conservatives, with 345 seats, achieved a sound overall majority, thus vindicating the anti-coalitionist stand of Bonar Law, and leaving Austen Chamberlain and his friends isolated, until in 1924 they crept back into Baldwin's government and reunited the party. 1922 therefore begins the long period of Tory domination that typified the inter-war years. Labour too, with 142 seats, had made a great electoral breakthrough, and since they now outnumbered the combined Liberal forces in the House of Commons, they became the official opposition and pushed the Liberals into third place in the party stakes. Within two years they were to form their first government.

The National Liberals suffered disastrously. They won 62 seats overall (compared with 136 won in 1918), but they lost 81; 39 of these, nearly all in industrial constituencies, were gained by Labour. Even the seats they did win (outside North Wales, their one region of independent strength) were only retained because of the lack of Conservative opposition. The Independent Liberals fared little better. They gained 43 seats, and ended up with 54 all told (compared with 28 in 1918); but they lost 14 seats, 9 to Labour, and fared particularly badly in the mining areas, once a stronghold of Liberalism. In fact, though the Asquithians won the occasional industrial seat, their main gains were in rural areas. Moreover, though they did well in constituencies where they faced only Conservatives or National Liberals, in three-cornered contests involving Labour their majorities in seats they did win were very small – an ominous sign for the future.

Thus the election of 1922 marked a further stage in the decline of the Liberal party. The party was still divided, and there was little sign of any renewed understanding between Asquith and Lloyd George. Both groups had lost important leaders: among the Coalitionists, Guest, Addison, Churchill and Greenwood had failed to retain their seats, as had the Asquithians, Runciman and Maclean. Most of these – with the notable exception of Addison, who joined the Labour party – ended up as real or crypto-Conservatives. In addition, many of the seats that were gained by the Liberals were held by small majorities, or were won as a result of special circumstances, such as the tactical withdrawal of the Conservatives from many constituencies fought by National Liberals, and the Asquithians' cashing in on the farmers' anti-Coalitionist protest vote in a number of rural seats. Above all, what the Liberals had failed to do was to ward off the challenge of Labour in terms of leadership, programme and electoral appeal. It was MacDonald who was now the hero of the industrial working classes, as Lloyd George had been little over a decade before; and it was Labour that was becoming *their* party, as the Liberals had been in an earlier generation. All this underlined the truth that the Liberals no longer had an obvious electoral base on which they could rely, and their very existence was now at stake. If they were to survive at all, let alone dislodge Labour from its position as the second party in the state, one thing was absolutely indispensable: the reconciliation of Asquith and Lloyd George.

4 Liberals United

Liberal reunion and the 1923 general election

Though, after the dismal results of the 1922 general election, the political reasons for the fusion of the Independent and National Liberals seemed overwhelming, the obstacles to reunion were profound. The crises and quarrels that had set Liberal against Liberal during the years between 1916 and 1922 could not easily be forgotten, and the personal relations of Asquith and Lloyd George were no better now than they had been during the years of coalition itself. For Asquith, the National Liberals were 'all of them renegades', and he indicated to Herbert Gladstone that 'he would never again accept Lloyd George as a colleague' (13). Yet what divided the two sections of Liberals was not just the personal pique and ambition of their leaders. From the Asquithian point of view it seemed on the morrow of the 1922 election that Lloyd George was not really prepared to break decisively with his former Conservative allies, or abandon completely the idea of a possible coalition; while some of his own followers – especially Guest, and Churchill with whom he remained on close terms – still hankered obsessively after some sort of anti-socialist centre party (**99**, V). Moreover Lloyd George gave no sign that he intended to wind up his own National Liberal organisation, or – an even greater irritant to the politically poverty-stricken Asquithians – relinquish his tight personal control over the bulging coffers of the Lloyd George Fund.

Asquith nevertheless accepted the principle of reunion, however reluctantly; but it was to be reunion on his terms. He made it clear that the ex-Coalitionists (especially Lloyd George) would be welcomed back to the Liberal party, not in a spirit of equality and friendship but as erring sinners who had repented of their folly and were now prepared to accept the wisdom and leadership of the Asquithian establishment. Asquith's followers (Maclean, Grey, Simon, Gladstone, Vivian Phillips, the new Chief Whip) were even more anti-Lloyd George than their chief. 'While my opinion is all for reunion', wrote Cowdray to Gladstone in December 1922, 'I consider, if reunion involved in any way our acceptance of Lloyd George, that we cannot

37

afford to pay such a price' (**98**). For these Liberals the re-entry of Lloyd George into the party on terms which would enable him to reassert his leadership, represented a threat to their status and influence, and to the old high-minded Liberal ideals which men like Herbert Gladstone personified and which Lloyd George despised.

For his part, Lloyd George became increasingly impressed with the advantages of reunion once he accepted the impossibility of 'coalition' or 'centre parties', and recognised the attenuation of his own National Liberal bloc and the growing power of the Labour party. But (as he said to C. P. Scott) though he was prepared 'to go a long way in the way of conciliation. . . . "I will not crawl. I will not crawl on my belly" ' (**13**). Hence his attempt in the spring of 1923, in a series of dramatic speeches throughout the country, to put himself over as the apostle of a revivified Liberalism, different from and superior to the orthodoxies of Conservatism and Socialism. His message was not very original. This was really a personal bid for power; an attempt to force himself on the Liberal party by asserting his own indispensability and thus achieving a reunified party, ultimately under his own leadership and control. This campaign worsened rather than allayed the fears of the Asquithians. Despite the considerable support for reunion in the constituencies, and among a large group of Liberal MPs in the Commons, the Asquithians were able to continue successfully their policy of paying lip service to reunion while doing little in practice to advance the cause. The attempt by the Welsh National Liberals to begin reunion in the Principality was rebuffed; while the Liberal party conference at Buxton in June reaffirmed its 'unabated confidence' in Asquith, and rejected the crucial amendment calling for discussions between the Independent and National Liberal leaders to discuss the best means of promoting party unity (**65**). This internal wrangling only worsened the Liberal position in the country, where there was a further decline in party morale and organisation, reflected in the poor Liberal by-election record in 1922–23 and the virtual collapse of Liberalism in the face of Labour in local elections in the great cities. 'If we do not reunite,' Lloyd George commented, 'Liberalism is done as a national driving force. For that reason I have welcomed every proposal for reunion put forward by Liberals of both sections, and I do not see what more I can do' (**63**). By the summer of 1923 little real progress had been made towards reunion. Only a political earthquake, it seemed, could overcome the suspicions and fears of both sides – and that was about to come.

In May 1923 Bonar Law, the Conservative Prime Minister, retired through ill-health and was succeeded by the Chancellor of the Exchequer, Stanley Baldwin. Baldwin came to the conclusion that the only cure for the country's economic ills, and particularly the grave problem of unemployment, was a policy of Protection. He decided, therefore, in accordance with his predecessor's undertaking, to obtain a mandate from the electorate before embarking on such a policy, and accordingly Parliament was to be dissolved and a general election held in December. It has been argued that Baldwin's motives were even more political than economic: the proposed general election was conceived primarily as a move against Lloyd George whose political stock was rising rapidly, partly as a result of a highly successful tour of the United States in September–November (**107**). More important, Baldwin apparently believed, on little real evidence, that Lloyd George was about to announce his conversion to a policy of Protection on his return to England, with all its dire implications for the unity of the Conservative party. Baldwin's famous Plymouth speech to the Party Conference in October, announcing his support for Protection, was therefore an attempt to preempt the issue and isolate Lloyd George; at the same time it would bind the ex-Coalitionist Conservative ministers firmly to the party. On the latter point Baldwin proved percipient; both Austen Chamberlain and Birkenhead supported him over Protection in the general election. But he completely misread Lloyd George's intentions. Conviction and self-interest (his attempt to rebuild his Liberal base) made Lloyd George a convinced if cool Free Trader, and on his arrival at Southampton on 9 November he condemned any new tariff policy [**doc. 8**].

This was the signal for Liberal reunion. The defence of Free Trade was a cause which all Asquithians could espouse wholeheartedly, and their hesitations of the previous two years were quickly forgotten in the general call to arms. On 13 November Lloyd George and his henchman, Sir Alfred Mond, met Asquith and Simon, and reunion was formally announced. A joint manifesto was then issued by the two leaders, Asquith and Lloyd George, for the coming general election, stressing the defence of Free Trade, though reference was also made to new policies for unemployment and foreign affairs. Agreement was reached on the selection of Liberal candidates in the constituencies, and in the end 454 were put forward, compared with 434 Labour candidates and 536 Conservatives; Lloyd George also agreed to contribute £90,000 to the Liberal election fund. Thus Stanley Baldwin achieved for the Liberals what they had been unable to achieve for themselves, and this was a reflection of the weaknesses of their new position.

It was the exigencies of the hour rather than any real union of hearts and minds among the Liberal leaders that produced the reconciliation of 1923. None of the long-term problems of the party – particularly the role of Lloyd George – were really solved, and the new Liberal unity came too late to help the party's electoral organisation in the constituencies. 'The apparent success of the Liberal reunion . . . was in fact only the signal for a much more bitter civil war within the party in 1924 than had been waged in 1923' (**98**). For the moment, however, the Liberals were passionately united in the defence of Free Trade as their main electoral slogan. Lloyd George in particular fought a vigorous campaign; he spoke all over the country and sat side by side with Asquith in the latter's constituency of Paisley. But even Lloyd George, though he also bitterly attacked Labour's proposal for a capital levy, was at one with Asquith and Grey in sticking mainly to the Protection issue. This meant that the Liberals were really fighting a negative and defensive campaign in favour of the economic *status quo*, and one that was directed primarily against the Tories rather than Labour, who (as in 1906) were as devoted Free Traders as themselves.

The results of the election were unexpected and unsatisfactory: for the Liberals, however, they were regarded as something of a triumph. One hundred and fifty-nine Liberals were returned, compared with 116 in 1922; though in fact they gained 83 new seats (since many of the former National Liberal seats that had depended upon Conservative votes were now lost), the majority, 67, from the Tories. Of these, 23 were gained in the boroughs, and 44 in the counties. It was this rural advance – largely at the expense of the Conservatives, though gains were also made from Labour – that formed the basis of the Liberal revival of 1923 (**63, 64**). That revival becomes even more impressive if one looks at the total votes cast, particularly in relation to the Labour party, and the pattern of Liberal voting. The total number of Liberal and Labour votes was very close (Liberal: 4,311, 147; Labour: 4,438, 508): the Liberals polled more votes in rural England than did Labour, and their continuing strength in much of Wales and Scotland meant that they remained the second party to the Conservatives in non-industrial Britain. Regionally, the Liberals' greatest gains were in the South-West; in parts of the Midlands and the North-West; and in East Anglia; though, rather freakishly, they also won some traditionally die-hard Tory boroughs such as Chichester, Aylesbury and Blackpool. The main factor at work here seems to have been the fear of rising prices that might follow from Protection, and worries about the government's failure to deal with unemployment (**94**).

There were features of the electoral results that were more disturbing for the Liberals. Sixty-eight seats were won in straight fights with Conservatives, and these would be at risk if Labour intervened in the

future, especially as more than 100 Liberal seats were gained with majorities of less than 2,000. Moreover, the Liberals won only 13 seats
from Labour and lost 23 to them, and even many of these gains were
due to local pacts with the Tories. Whatever their success in rural
England in 1923, the Liberal cause in industrial England was
retreating even further before the advance of Labour, and it was the
challenge of Labour rather than the hoary issue of Free Trade that was
the vital one for the Liberal party. Since Labour's vote was concentrated in the right places it gained 191 seats, but the Conservatives,
with 258 seats, still remained the largest party, though they lacked an
overall majority in the House of Commons. The Liberals were
therefore pushed decisively into third place, thus ensuring that they
now suffered, as Labour had done before 1914, from the inbuilt bias of
the electoral system against third parties. This was the electoral trap
from which the Liberals ever since have been unable to escape. In
many ways, therefore, the Liberal revival of 1923 was insecure, and
the general election of that year marks another stage in the party's
decline.

That election was also important for the internal balance of power
within the Liberal party. The followers of Lloyd George did particularly badly; nearly half of them lost their seats, and this included
Churchill, Mond, Hamar Greenwood and McCurdy. By contrast
Herbert Gladstone calculated that 118 out of the 191 Asquithians
who stood were returned to the House of Commons. This inevitably
gave a fillip to Asquith's leadership at the expense of Lloyd George, a
fact that was to be of enormous importance when the new parliament
met and the Liberals were faced with the agonising task of deciding
whether and under what circumstances they should allow Labour to
form a government.

Liberals and the first Labour government

As the leader of the largest party, Stanley Baldwin continued in office
and faced the House of Commons when it reassembled in January in
1924. Since, however, the results of the recent election could be interpreted as a clear vote against the Prime Minister's policy of Protection,
the Liberals were prepared to cooperate with their Free Trade allies in
the Labour party in ousting the Conservatives (which was accomplished on 21 January) and allowing Ramsay MacDonald to form the first
Labour government. One historian of the Liberal party comments:
'Asquith rejected the idea of playing for a Liberal administration. Why
he did so must remain a mystery; and it is arguable that this decision

was the most disastrous single action ever performed by a Liberal towards his Party' (**69**). This presupposes for Asquith much more freedom of action than in fact he possessed. Though he toyed with various paper schemes for getting the Liberals into office there and then, all suffered from the fatal flaw that they must inevitably depend on Conservative support, and that was anathema to the Liberal rank-and-file. Besides, Baldwin himself was unwilling to cooperate in any plan which prevented Labour being given its rightful chance to form a government, a view which was shared by the King. In effect, Asquith and Lloyd George felt the same. Asquith made no attempt to push himself forward in opposition to MacDonald, and the Liberal leaders' decision to support a Labour administration had the strong backing of the party in the country [**doc. 9a**].

That decision was of course determined as much by party advantage as by their sense of 'fair play' or constitutional rectitude. Asquith and Lloyd George differed considerably, however, over what constituted party advantage. For Asquith, the Labour government should be supported only until it had made the inevitable mess of things, since he believed firmly that Labour was 'unfit to govern'; power would then devolve once more into his own experienced hands. The best policy for the Liberals, therefore, was to adopt a cautious and detached attitude towards the new ministry, so as not to be implicated in its failures and unpopularity and thus spoil their own chances of assuming office. As Asquith told the Liberal Parliamentary Party, the experiment 'could hardly be tried under safer conditions . . . it is we, if we really understand our business, who really control the situation' (**63**). The Labour government was thus to be supported by the Liberals (as Lenin said on another occasion) 'as a rope supports a hanging man'.

Lloyd George, on the other hand, wanted a real policy of cooperation with Labour in order to carry through 'a full harvest of Radical reform'. Such a programme could be supported not only on its merits, but because, if successful, the Liberals would inevitably gain from the accompanying *kudos*. Moreover, it would be a truly *Liberal* rather than Socialist programme, since (as Lloyd George rightly saw) MacDonald had neither the will nor the parliamentary strength to carry through a policy of full-blooded Socialism. The outcome of this collaboration, therefore, would be to make Liberalism once more a vital popular creed in the country at the expense of the Labour party. In addition, since the programme would be based on the radical Liberalism that Lloyd George himself now personified, it would increase his own prestige within the party and render the position of Asquith and his friends increasingly insecure [**doc. 9b**]. Once more for the Welshman policy and power were to go hand in hand. Yet he had his doubts. Lloyd George would have liked some sort of pact with Labour before putting them in office, though in the end he went along with Asquith's unconditional policy. But, as he grumbled to Scott a few weeks after MacDonald became Premier (correctly as it turned out): 'If Labour succeeds they get all the credit; if it fails we get the blame for putting them in power' (**13**).

The strategy of both Liberal leaders in January 1924 depended ultimately on the cooperation of the Labour party; and, given its weak parliamentary position, how could it not accept the proffered assistance? Astonishingly, Labour rejected it vehemently. Indeed, the government and its supporters redoubled their attacks on the Liberals – and especially on Lloyd George – both inside and outside the House of Commons in the most bitter and virulent terms, and continued to assail them in the constituencies and at by-elections even if (as at Oxford in the summer) it meant letting in a Tory. 'Requiring active Liberal support to retain office Labour responded not by conciliating, or even ignoring the Liberals, but by seeking to pulverise them' (**94**). Yet the writing had been on the wall for some time.

Since the coupon election at least, the Labour leadership had made no secret of its conviction that the key to Labour advance lay in the destruction of the Liberal party's credibility as a radical party of the Left and as an alternative government. Hence '. . . the purpose of the first Labour Government was not legislation, but the assertion of the party's maturity, fitness to govern, and independence of the Liberals' (**98**). To cooperate with the Liberals meant accepting their right to exist and compete on equal terms with Labour for the working-class vote; even perhaps becoming subordinate to them, as they had been before and during the war. The Parliamentary Labour Party would no longer be patronised by (in the cutting words of one Labour historian) 'the party of the self consciously superior, the rich and clever lawyers, the effortless Oxford men' (**39**). MacDonald's aim, therefore, was to keep the Liberals at arm's length and, by pursuing a policy of responsible government and moderate reform, to underline even more clearly their total irrelevance in the British political system. The *coup de grâce* was then to be administered by dissolving Parliament at the worst possible moment for the Liberal party's electoral prospects. Hence 'the 1924 Parliament . . . existed only as an armed truce between general elections' (**98**).

Labour's refusal to cooperate meant that the Liberals lost all freedom of manoeuvre in the House of Commons. They were caught in the trap they themselves had helped to create, since they had either to support Labour's policies positively in the lobbies (mere abstention might be insufficient to prevent a Labour defeat), or vote against them with the Conservatives and bring about another general election for which they were totally unprepared. The demoralising effects of this unhappy position came out in the Liberals' attitude towards government legislation. 'In the lobbies, the party presented a picture of total confusion and inconsistency' (**63**). The Liberals voted three ways early in the session in the 'Poplar' debate (concerned with the amount of relief to be paid by Boards of Guardians) as indeed they did a few months later on the government's Eviction Bill. Over the ministry's proposals to discontinue support for the Singapore naval base, similarly, the majority of Liberals voted with the government, but some supported the Conservative censure motion, and some abstained. When, in May, Lloyd George hoped to launch an outright attack on the government's unemployment policies, he found that Asquith (with the support of most of the parliamentary party) was unprepared to vote against MacDonald on the issue, and Lloyd George had to content himself with abstention. The last crumb of comfort disappeared for the Liberals when the proposed Electoral Reform Bill (which would have given some measure of proportional representation) was destroyed by an alliance of Tories and Labour backbenchers. Labour, it seemed, would concede nothing. As Lloyd George said bitterly but correctly: 'Liberals are to be the oxen to drag the Labour wain over the rough roads of Parliament . . . and . . . when there is no further use for them, they are to be slaughtered. That is the Labour idea of cooperation' (**98**).

At the same time as they were struggling to resolve the problems caused by their relations with Labour, the Liberals were faced with their own internal problems, exacerbated now by the tensions and frustrations of their parliamentary position. The most obvious of these was their lack of a firm united leadership. Though their personal relations were reasonably cordial, there was no real political harmony between the two Liberal leaders, especially since Asquith's complacency was nourished by the relative success of his own followers in the recent election compared with the decimation of Lloyd George's National Liberals. Asquith's henchmen were as suspicious and distrustful of Lloyd George as ever, still determined to keep him in a subordinate position in the party and, if possible, to block his eventual succession to the leadership. 'They have no desire', wrote one Liberal observer, 'except to strangle him at the earliest possible opportunity' (**63**). This distrust was worsened by disputes between the party officials and Lloyd George over money, since the Liberal party, lacking the obvious resources of its two rivals, was in a near-bankrupt financial position, having already borne the heavy expense of two recent general elections, with another one likely in the near future. Yet money was the key to a more effective party organisation and an increase in the number of Liberal candidates, an absolute necessity if the party was to have any chance of improving its position at the next election.

Since Lloyd George was known to command ample funds, should he not, argued men like Gladstone and Maclean, place them at the disposal of the party of which he was now a leading member, and at the same time disband his own shadowy National Liberal organisation? 'There must be a marriage settlement', wrote Gladstone. 'The only thing he can give us, has got to give, is £.s.d., and we cannot give him everything for nothing'. 'L. G', wrote another Asquithian, 'needs to join up with us far more than we need to join up with him' (**98**). Their arguments were impeccable in strict party terms. But for Lloyd George, his Fund was the one material weapon he had against the Liberal 'old gang', and why should he hand it over to prop up the power and the outworn ideas of his political enemies? Better to hang on to it until the party was ready to accept him as leader, and then use it for his own radical purposes. So far as the 'marriage settlement' was concerned, Lloyd George played a waiting game in the early months of the Labour Government, much to the fury of Gladstone and Maclean. The acrimonious negotiations over how much cash Lloyd George should provide for the party funds wound on fruitlessly into the summer, poisoning any real accord among the party leaders, and leaving the Liberal faithful in the constituencies to drift along helplessly or give up in despair. And once again these weaknesses were reflected in a series of poor by-election results (**26**). The Liberals lost only one seat (at Oxford) during the lifetime of the first Labour government, but the results showed quite clearly the continuous advance of Labour into Liberal territory, and a Conservative revival, and thus foreshadowed the general election of 1924.

Even if the practical problems of leadership, finance and organisation had been solved, the Liberals were still faced with the more imponderable question, one which has haunted them ever since: what did Liberalism stand for? What original solutions could Liberals provide to the economic and social problems of the time? To these questions there were no obvious answers. Certainly, under Asquith's supine leadership the party lacked any clear distinctive doctrine which could appeal to the working-class electorate, as indeed its disarray in the face of Labour's legislative proposals showed. As many observers noted, there was little now to distinguish the attitudes of moderate Labour from those of radical Liberals. In the early days of his government at least, MacDonald's policy of preempting Liberalism (Snowden's Budget was Gladstonian in every line) seemed to be working. 'Ramsay MacDonald is definitely established', wrote one Liberal, 'as the national leader of the Left. . . . he will take with him a very large section of the Liberal party when next he goes to the country' (**63**). This seemed not unlikely. The weaknesses of Asquith's leadership and traditional Liberalism came out all too clearly in the lacklustre character of the party conference in May 1924. By contrast, Lloyd George, in speeches and in a series of investigations and reports which he organised with little reference to the party hierarchy, was adumbrating a bolder Liberal programme, a forerunner of the famous coloured books of 1925–28. 'I've fought him as hard as anyone', wrote C. F. G. Masterman to his wife, 'but I have to confess when Ll. G. came back to the party, ideas came back to the party' (**98**).

By the spring of 1924 Lloyd George was increasingly disillusioned with the attempted policy of cooperation with Labour, and indeed with the state of the Liberal party itself. Both problems could be dealt with, he believed, by adopting a policy of all-out opposition to the Labour government. Even if this led directly to a general election, the traumatic shock thus administered to the Liberal party would, whatever the final electoral results, be salutary, and pave the way for his own take-over. In March, suddenly and dramatically, he dissolved the old National Liberal organisation, thus severing one more link with his Coalitionist past. In the course of the next few months he assailed the government's foreign and domestic policies, and in a series of caustic speeches denounced Labour's view of the Liberals as mere 'lobby fodder' and urged his fellow MPs to vote against government Bills. This was in fact done by some Liberals over both the naval estimates and the Eviction Bill; but, as we have seen, his proposal to vote against the government's unemployment policies in May went unsupported by Asquith and the bulk of the parliamentary party. Since Asquith was unprepared as yet to overthrow Labour, Lloyd George came to feel during the summer that only by collusion with the Conservatives could he achieve his aim. They, for their part, reunited under Baldwin, who had by now abandoned Protection, and with their organisation in good trim, looked forward eagerly to the next general election.

All the signs indicated that an election could not be far away. The Liberal officials therefore made another attempt to bring negotiations with Lloyd George to a head, and prepare the party for the coming contest. Herbert Gladstone, as party manager, had always insisted that the

Liberals should run at least 500 candidates at the next election, which would mean raising about £200,000. But Lloyd George, employing his usual delaying tactics, insisted first that a committee on party reorganisation be set up, and when it reported, refused to accept its recommendations over the number of candidates. Why should he alone be expected to finance the Liberal electoral effort? It was not until the beginning of October, only a few days before the government fell, that he finally agreed to contribute just £50,000 to the Liberal election fund, saying blithely to Maclean: 'Why should we have more than 300 candidates?' (**69**). In the end 340 were put forward, compared with 453 in 1923. Gladstone believed that Lloyd George's parsimony was deliberate: an attempt to destroy the Liberal party at the polls, so that he could pick up the pieces later. Indeed, there is much to be said for the view that Lloyd George believed that a Liberal defeat was certain, and was reluctant to waste his resources in supporting hopeless candidates. Nor, perhaps, was he entirely unhappy at the prospect of a small Liberal group in the House of Commons, purged of its Asquithian elements, holding the balance of power and looking to him for salvation.

On 2 October Lloyd George wrote to his daughter, Megan: 'It looks now as if we were in for another General Election. I have done my best to precipitate it' (**9**). This situation had come about as a result of the government's policy towards the Soviet Union. In August MacDonald (who had already recognised the Bolshevik government) aimed at settling the outstanding differences between the two countries by negotiating a series of Anglo-Soviet treaties. The most controversial proposal was that of a British loan to Russia, to be linked with a vague Soviet agreement to provide compensation for British bond-holders whose claims had been wiped out during the Revolution. Lloyd George decided to oppose the treaty, and use his opposition to force the Liberals to join with the Conservatives in ousting Labour. Most Liberals, including Asquith, agreed at a party meeting on 1 October to follow Lloyd George's lead. It was therefore their Russian policy that was the real cause of the Labour government's downfall. The actual occasion, however, was the famous 'Campbell Case' which arose out of a proposed governmental prosecution of J. R. Campbell, a leading Communist, for seditious writings. The case was taken up and then dropped by the government, and as a result the Conservatives tabled a motion of censure. The Liberals, however, disconcerted by what they regarded as really a 'red herring', moved an amendment calling for a Committee of Inquiry into the whole affair, hoping in this way to bury the problem and return to the original bone of contention – the Soviet treaty. MacDonald riposted by making the amendment a vote of confidence. The Tories then abandoned their own motion and voted with the Liberals for the crucial amendment, thus bringing about the defeat of the government on 8 October, and a general election at the end of the month.

Lloyd George was hoist with his own petard: he got his election – but at the wrong time and on the wrong issue. Instead of fighting it, as he had hoped, on the feeble record of the Labour government (compared with his own vigorous radicalism), the issues were clouded by the miasma of 'anti-Communism' arising from the government's Soviet policy, plus the 'Campbell Case' and (to some extent) the notorious 'Zinoviev Letter'. The electorate was thus polarised, and not only did the official Liberal message (over-cautious anyway) go largely unheeded amid the clash of the big party battalions, but many electors who had voted Liberal in 1923 now fled for the safety of the Tory camp. The Liberals thus paid dearly for their support for a Labour government ten months before. In any case, the configuration of the results was decided by the simple fact that the Liberals put up only 340 candidates, due not only to lack of money, but to the general collapse of Liberal organisation and morale in the constituencies. By contrast, Labour's vigour still remained astonishingly high, and it now fought on a wider front with just over 500 candidates – about 100 more than in 1923. The Conservative party, united and confident once again in its defence of the *status quo*, fielded 552 candidates.

The outcome of the election was a clear victory for the Conservatives, who gained 412 seats, while Labour emerged with 151 seats. The Liberals were massacred, and reduced to a mere 40 MPs. They lost no less than 105 seats to the Tories. All the Liberal gains made in rural and middle-class constituencies in 1923 were completely wiped out; and their situation in the urban areas was not much better – only 6 Liberal MPs survived to represent the 11 greatest cities. Hardly any Liberal leaders except Lloyd George, Mond and Simon escaped disaster; even Asquith lost his seat at Paisley. The long-term consequences were profound. The Conservatives won the election; but Labour, though it had 40 fewer seats than in 1923, increased its poll by more than a million votes, thus retaining control of a secure and indeed expanding electoral base. More important, it achieved triumphantly its main aim – the destruction of the Liberal party as a major rival on the left and as an alternative party of government. In that sense Labour, no less than the Tories, was the victor in 1924. 'We are', lamented Asquith, 'a dying party, set between the upper and the nether millstones' (**63**).

5 Lloyd George as Liberal Leader

Lloyd George takes over

The shock of the 1924 general election did little to make the Liberals face the realities of their political position. The fundamental problems of leadership, organisation, finance and policy still remained; and so far as the party hierarchy was concerned the Liberals were now even more disunited than before. Asquith's hold over the parliamentary party became increasingly tenuous since he was now raised to the peerage and sat in the House of Lords as Lord Oxford; while a majority of the tiny group of Liberal MPs (unlike the situation in 1923) were ex-Coalitionists, sympathetic to Baldwin's Conservative government. Asquith's supporters still remained hostile to Lloyd George, as determined as ever to prevent him emerging as party leader, and seeing him as 'immeasurably the greatest obstacle to Liberal progress' (**98**). They failed, however, to prevent Lloyd George being elected Chairman of the Parliamentary Liberal Party by thirty-six votes to seven. The Asquithian minority in the House of Commons, under Runciman's leadership, expressed their displeasure by forming the so-called 'Radical Group', 'radical' only in the Pickwickian sense that they were determined to oppose both the Conservative government and the Labour party, and thus prepare for the next electoral battle.

This meant, as always, money; and therefore raised once again for the Asquithian party managers the distasteful topic of the Lloyd George Fund. Faced with a desperate financial position both at headquarters and in the constituencies, the need for a large long-term income for the party was plain for all to see. But on the thorny question of using the Fund to rescue the party from impending bankruptcy, the attitude of both sides had advanced not a jot since the discussions that had preceded the 1924 election. 'His money was got in unholy ways', complained Gladstone, 'but what earthly right has he got to the exclusive use of it?' (**98**). Lloyd George remained, however, as full of excuses and as reluctant to contribute to an Asquithian-controlled party exchequer as ever; he would be 'a bloody lunatic' to do so exclaimed his Labour friend, Jimmy Thomas, and besides he had other political uses for the money. The new Liberal Administrative Committee therefore launched the 'Million Pound Fund' at the beginning of 1925 to make the party financially self-supporting. The scheme had some success at a local level but overall it was a dismal failure and only served to reveal to the country at large the true plight of the Liberal party. This failure also increased the Asquithians' resentment of Lloyd George – especially since he was now planning to spend £240,000 on his Land League – but made them more dependent on his charity. The price demanded by Lloyd George for any future help was in effect the Liberal party's support for his 'land campaign'.

This campaign was begun in September 1925 with a brilliant opening speech by Lloyd George at a rally in the West country, a prelude to the publication in the following month of *The Land and the Nation*, known popularly as the 'Green Book'. This trenchant report was the result of a private investigation into the ownership and use of rural land, supported and financed by Lloyd George, without reference to Asquith. The Green Book argued that private landlordism was unable to provide an efficient and prosperous agricultural system: state help was needed to remedy its deficiencies. Lloyd George did not support land nationalisation, but he did propose that the state take over control of the soil and through a series of local committees impose the reforms that were needed, and thus help to revivify the economy generally. Lloyd George's land campaign was a tribute to his long-standing support for rural radicalism which went back to the very beginnings of his political career (**100**). More important, it also marked for him the beginnings of a new creative period in policy-making after the uncertainties of the post-war years, and this new self-confidence took him back once more to the centre of the political stage. Lloyd George was moving to the left; and it is significant that his blistering attacks on the government's economic policies in 1925–26 made him in many ways the hero of the Labour party, in marked contrast to their derision of him during the parliament of 1924. In all this he hoped to take the Liberal party with him and commit it to a definite non-socialist but radical role, sustained by his money and his leadership.

The major proposals in the Green Book, however, were not greeted with any great enthusiasm by the Liberal party. Many members looked askance at its quasi-nationalisation programme, and it was indeed on this issue that Sir Alfred Mond (a leading ex-Coalitionist) finally left the party and joined the Conservatives. Nevertheless, early in 1926 Lloyd George went ahead and formed the 'Land and Nation League' to campaign for his land reforms, without obtaining official party endorsement, supported lavishly (as we have seen) from his own private fund. Asquith deprecated this action in a mild letter to his Liberal rival as likely to increase party disunity. Despite the consternation of his supporters he was unprepared as yet to seek an open confrontation with Lloyd George. The latter, for his part, was eventually prepared to modify his land proposals, and as a result they were finally accepted as party policy at the Land Convention held in February 1926. This was in its way a joint success for both Liberal leaders. For Asquith it was his last. Within three months the quarrels over the General Strike had shattered the fragile accord that he had built up with Lloyd George and led, unexpectedly, to his own downfall as Liberal leader.

Both Liberal statesmen firmly supported the government in the stand it took against the TUC's resort to a General Strike in support of the miners on 3 May. But whereas Asquith refused to contemplate any criticism of the government in the midst of what he regarded as a 'constitutional' crisis, and supported wholeheartedly Baldwin's policy of unconditional surrender, Lloyd George believed that he was fully justified in emphasising the government's own responsibility for the strike, and argued in favour of 'negotiated compromise' [**doc. 10a**]. Lloyd George dramatised his differences with his leader by ostentatiously refusing to attend a meeting of the Liberal Shadow Cabinet on 10 May, adding in a letter to Godfrey Collins, the Chief Whip, 'I prefer the Liberal policy of trusting to conciliation rather than to force' (**198**). This was followed up by a more detailed exposition of his views in an article published in the American press. It was this eminently sensible article that became for Asquith the final straw in his relationship with Lloyd George [**doc. 10b**]. On 20 May (after the General Strike was over) Asquith sent Lloyd George a stinging rebuke for absenting himself on 'wholly inadequate grounds' from the Shadow Cabinet meeting, and sent it to the press. 'At last', wrote Maclean expectantly to Gladstone, 'I think the break has come' (**198**). Lloyd George replied, however, in a mild and conciliatory spirit – his original letter was largely rewritten by C. P. Scott. Nevertheless, Asquith, spurred on by the mounting extremism of his Shadow Cabinet colleagues, determined to bring matters to a head and secure the resignation of Lloyd George. But, as Frances Stevenson noted: 'He will not resign. His tactics are perfect. He is giving them a long rope with which to hang themselves . . . ' (**11**).

And so it turned out. To carry through his plans Asquith needed the support of the national party organisations: in June, on this issue at least, they rallied in support of Lloyd George. They seem to have felt that Asquith was acting precipitately and unreasonably in trying to force Lloyd George's resignation without fair warning; while on the wider issue of the leaders' attitude to the General Strike it now appeared that Lloyd George had adopted a truly Liberal attitude, while Asquith had truckled to the Tory diehards. It is clear that Asquith had misjudged the temper of the party. He was in fact taken ill while these party discussions took place, but since he had indicated that he would not 'continue to hold the leadership for a day' unless his policies were endorsed by the party, he resigned the leadership at the earliest possible moment after he was well again, in October 1926. 'The end of Asquith's leadership had been a painful and protracted business. He had stayed too long in an impossible situation; believing, falsely, that the Liberal Party could be revived by its old leaders . . .' (**103**). In February 1928 he died.

Thus Lloyd George at last entered on his inheritance. He remained only *de facto* leader, but the reality of his power was seen in the destruction of the dominant position of the Asquithian 'old gang' in the party machine. Sir Robert Hutchinson (a Lloyd George man) became Chief Whip; and after much heart-searching by the Administrative Committee, Vivian Phillips was pushed out as Chairman of the party organisation in return for Lloyd George's agreement to finance 500 candidates at the next general election. Sir Herbert Samuel (newly returned from his post as High Commissioner in Palestine) then became a 'neutral' Chairman — a judicious and successful appointment. The leading Asquithians (Phillips, Hudson, Grey, Runciman, Gladstone) retired into a new 'cave of Adullum' by forming the 'Liberal Council' to defend true Liberalism, though they were animated primarily by personal animus towards Lloyd George. It remained an irrelevant and out-of-date body. Lloyd George had thus dealt successfully with the immediate problems of leadership, organisation and finance. A Liberal revival seemed to be on the way with the winning of two by-elections (Southwark and Bosworth) in the spring of 1927. He could now turn his attention to his major interest — policy.

Lloyd George had already seized the initiative in the field of policy-making with the publication two years earlier of the Green Book on land reform. He now hoped to do the same for British industry. He therefore gave encouragement and support to the ideas on industrial reorganisation which were being worked out by a group of Liberal intellectuals led by Ramsay Muir, Walter Layton and Ernest Simon, all of whom were associated with the Liberal Summer Schools which began in 1921. Even more important was the fact that J. M. Keynes, who was just beginning to develop his revolutionary theories on finance and employment, became associated with the Summer

Schools, and through them he resumed his association with Lloyd George, which had been damaged by the publication in 1919 of *The Economic Consequences of the Peace*. Keynes had no patience with the Liberal leader's emphasis on rural reconstruction. But the two men had a common concern with the problem of unemployment. It was partly as a result of the Cambridge economist's influence, therefore, that Lloyd George agreed to finance a Liberal inquiry organised by Keynes and his friends (Lloyd George himself chaired the committee on unemployment) into the country's industrial problems (**102**). Their report was published as *Britain's Industrial Future* (the 'Yellow Book') in February 1928. It argued in favour of an expansionist economic policy financed by the state through a National Investment Board and a vast public works programme, accompanied by monetary controls and the curbing of monopolies. This would help to stimulate industry and employment. The sophisticated economic analysis of the report was neither understood nor welcomed by public opinion. But it has been described by one historian as 'the most far-sighted policy document produced by any political party between the wars' (**98**), a judgement that has been endorsed by others (**50**).

1928 was thus a fruitful year for the Liberal party. The new enthusiasm seemed to be reflected also in two more by-election gains (Lancaster and St Ives), causing Lloyd George to reflect on the Liberals' political future and particularly the difficult problem of relations with the Labour party. Despite the euphoria produced by the by-election results since Lloyd George had taken over as leader, these Liberal victories were in rural seats, and Labour (which won twelve by-elections between 1924 and 1929) was still the main beneficiary of Conservative unpopularity. 'We will fight the general election,' Lloyd George proclaimed at that year's party conference, 'as an independent party, and we will act together in the next parliament as an independent party' (**98**). Brave words. But everything depended on the ability of the Liberal party to make a real recovery at the next election, which could not be far away. With a strong leader, an original programme, and more than 500 candidates in the field, the Liberals now had no excuse for failure. It would be, as Lloyd George rightly observed, 'a last throw for the Liberal Party' (**98**).

Defeat and dissension

Even before it was announced that the general election would be held in May 1929 Lloyd George had launched the Liberal campaign with the publication in March of a sixpenny pamphlet, *We Can Conquer*

Unemployment. This presented in a more popular form the 'public works' proposals of the Yellow Book, and argued that through a vast building programme of roads and houses 600,000 men could be put to work at a cost to the country of £250 million [**doc. 11**]. Indeed Lloyd George went further and pledged that, if the Liberals were returned to power, unemployment would be drastically reduced within one year. The Conservatives, sticking to their policy of 'safety first', dismissed the Liberal programme as unworkable; Labour, nonplussed, argued that the Liberals had purloined their own ideas. 'The Liberal Party has secured the ear of the nation,' asserted Lloyd George, and even the Asquithians supported the 'pledge', though they had private reservations about its feasibility. Lloyd George thus dominated the Liberal campaign until polling took place on 30 May (*Can Lloyd George do it?*, asked the economists Henderson and Keynes in a sympathetic pamphlet); and an additional fillip was given to the Liberals' enthusiasm by their victory at two more by-elections, Eddisbury and Holland-with-Boston. This marks 'the Indian summer of the old Liberal party' (**94**).

Yet though the Liberal leaders – particularly Samuel – worked hard to get their message on unemployment across to the public, they largely failed. In the end Labour, with 288 seats, emerged as the largest party; the Conservatives won 260 seats, and the Liberals trailed well behind with only 59. Once again, nearly all the seats they did win were from Conservatives and in rural constituencies, mainly in the traditional Liberal areas of the 'Celtic Fringe', the West country and East Anglia. They made no advance in industrial areas, and indeed lost ground to Labour in North-East Yorkshire, Lancashire and East London. It is true that the Liberals could point to the fact that they had polled over five million votes (23 per cent of the total compared with 17 per cent in 1924) and this strengthened their commitment to electoral reform. But the basic fact remained that they had thrown all their resources into the 1929 election and were probably better prepared from every point of view than in any other post-war election. Yet the end result was that they gained only nineteen more seats than in 1924, and, as the National Liberal Federation (NLF) said, it was 'a lost battle in view of our hopes and aims' (**94**). It was not just that the Liberal programme was not treated with the attention it deserved – that is the fate of all party programmes; nor that the electorate was profoundly sceptical about the sincerity of Lloyd George's promises over unemployment and the new-found unity among the Liberal leaders. Rather it was that the Liberals fought as a third party and were regarded as a third party; in particular, they were unable to damage the now traditional commitment of the industrial working classes to the Labour party which had been built up since the First World War, partly as a result of the Liberals' own mistakes. The 1929 general election therefore represents the end of the road for the Liberal party as far as their attempt to reemerge as a potential party of government is concerned.

Between the election of 1929 and the political crisis of 1931, the story of the Liberal party is one of further frustration, disappointment, and a relapse into disunity. The Liberals were faced once more with financial hardship, since Lloyd George, sticking strictly to the agreement of 1926, was no longer prepared to support the party from his private Fund, and this soon produced the all-too-familiar consequences of disintegrating organisation and dwindling candidatures. But the main problem for the Liberals lay, once again, in relations with Labour. If, as Marx suggests, all great events in history occur twice 'the first time as tragedy, the second as farce', this perhaps applies to the Liberals' record during the first and second Labour governments. It is true that in 1929 they were spared the responsibility for putting Labour into office, since Baldwin resigned before Parliament met. Unlike 1924 too, they could at least abstain without necessarily imperilling the life of the government. But the Liberals were unable to avoid the further duty of deciding whether and under what conditions to keep Labour in power.

At first Lloyd George aimed at a policy of parliamentary independence, judging Labour's proposals on their merits and if necessary abstaining or even voting against them. Above all, party unity was to be maintained. This policy soon collapsed when the Parliamentary Liberal Party twice voted three ways over the government's Coal Bill in 1929–30. From mid-1930 Lloyd George began to move towards a policy of real cooperation with Labour in order to achieve an agreed policy on unemployment, and electoral reform. This policy was successful insofar as the Labour leaders, whose self-confidence was being sapped by their inability to deal effectively with the unemployment problem, were prepared to enter into discussions with the Liberal leader (**50**). Indeed, faced with this intractable problem and under bitter attack in the House of Commons from the opposition and his own left-wing over the mounting unemployment figures, MacDonald appealed for support to the leaders of the other two parties. Baldwin, unwilling to prop up the government, refused, but Lloyd George agreed. The discussions that followed over the next year between Liberal and Labour representatives were friendly, but in the end abortive, since MacDonald was not really prepared to accept Liberal proposals on economic policy and, owing to party opposition, was unable to concede their demand for proportional representation (**106**).

Lloyd George's policy of cooperation with Labour had in any case its own internal dangers for the Liberal party, as events soon showed. In November 1930 five Liberals, led by Simon and Hutchinson, defied the party agreement to abstain and supported a Tory amendment to the King's Speech. This was followed by Hutchinson's resignation as Chief Whip. Simon, increasingly antipathetic to his leader's policy, gradually moved towards the Conservative camp [**doc. 12**]. In June 1931 he and his followers finally resigned the Liberal Whip, and formed a group calling themselves the Liberal Nationals. Lloyd George had meanwhile continued his meetings with MacDonald, and though he had protested to the Liberal Candidates Association at the end of 1930 that 'there is no deal and no pact', he now became increasingly pro-Labour, seeing the Labour party as the only possible bulwark against the growing clamour for Protection. In fact it seems possible that in the spring of 1931 MacDonald was considering inviting Lloyd George and a number of other Liberals to join his Cabinet (**98, 106**). This enticing prospect came to nothing, since in July Lloyd George was taken seriously ill and was therefore out of active politics during the dramatic events of August 1931 which saw the split in the Labour Cabinet over cuts in unemployment pay, MacDonald's resignation, and the subsequent formation of a National Government under his leadership, consisting of representatives of all three parties but opposed by the overwhelming majority of the Labour party (**16**).

Lloyd George supported the formation of the National Government, and encouraged leading Liberals to accept office in it. Samuel and Lord Reading became members of the Cabinet as Home Secretary and Foreign Secretary respectively, and a number of other Liberals were also appointed. It was assumed that Lloyd George himself would eventually enter the Cabinet when his health had recovered. Superficially the Liberals' policy had attractions: it gave them office, it papered over the growing fissures within the Parliamentary Party, and it avoided, seemingly, the prospect of facing an immediate general election in which, given their feeble by-election record over the previous two years, they were bound to do badly. On this last point they were soon disenchanted, for the Conservatives, rightly confident of their ability to dominate a new House of Commons, insisted on an early general election, backed by the Liberal Nationals, and MacDonald's own parliamentary position was now too weak to enable him to resist.

The Liberals were caught in a Tory trap. If they supported the National Government in the forthcoming general election, in opposition to Labour, they would become the accessories of the Conservatives in a new 'coupon' election, which would mean (as Lloyd George pointed out) 'signing the death warrant of the Liberal Party as a separate party' (**98**); if they went into opposition they would be destroyed at the polls. In the end they got the worst of all possible worlds. The Conservatives obtained their election in October, but Samuel and his Liberal colleagues refused to resign, much to the disgust of Lloyd George. From his sickbed the Liberal leader denounced their action, in effect broke with them and the Liberal party, and advocated support for Labour – the only independent Free Trade party left to vote for. The Liberals were now in a desperate position to fight an election. Not only were there just 160 candidates all told, but they fought as three groups: the Liberal Nationals, basically pro-Conservative; the miniscule Lloyd George group, who were pro-Labour; and the Samuelite Liberals, who were non-Conservative and anti-Labour. To add insult to injury, the Conservatives, who were now virtually unassailable, put up candidates against the five Liberal ministers, despite the fact that they supported the same government; the Liberal National candidates, by contrast, were generally unopposed.

The general election of 1931 was a triumph for the Conservative party (disguised as the National Government), a disaster for Labour, and a humiliation for the Liberals. The Conservatives won 473 seats, Labour was reduced to 52 MPs, and the Liberals had 72 seats. But this last figure meant little, since the Simonite bloc of 35 MPs were now virtually Conservative supporters; and, significantly, the Liberal vote fell by more than 3 million. Lloyd George, now head of a tiny family clan of 4 independent Liberal MPs, definitely gave up the Liberal leadership, saying that he was 'completely at variance with the disastrous course into which the party has been guided' (**69**). He was succeeded by Samuel, who still clung limpet-like to office, though his colleagues, Reading and Crewe, retired; this enabled Simon at last to reap his reward for his nice timing by being appointed Foreign Secretary. With the inevitable introduction of a policy of Protection by the government in the spring of 1932, the position of the Free Trade ministers became increasingly untenable; and though at first there was an 'agreement to differ' with their Protectionist colleagues, growing pressure from the Liberal party brought to an end an indefensible situation (**10**). Samuel and his colleagues resigned from the government in September, and the Liberals eventually joined Labour on the opposition benches. By that time the Simonite Liberals had travelled even further in the opposite direction and tightened their links with the Conservative party.

The general election of 1935 drove home in brutal fashion the implications of these events for the Liberals. Though the National

Government (now patently Conservative under Baldwin's leadership) easily won, Labour regained about 100 seats and most of its leaders returned to the House of Commons. The Liberals were reduced to the paltry total of 21 MPs. Once 'the great Liberal party', they were now a tiny minority on the sidelines of British politics. So they have remained.

Part Three: Assessment

For recent historians the debate on the causes of Liberal decline revolves around two interrelated themes: first, the relations between the Liberal and Labour parties, particularly during the Edwardian period, as it is then that some historians discern the beginnings of Labour's successful challenging of the Liberals' command of the working-class vote; second, the impact of the First World War, which other historians regard as the primary cause of the decline of the Liberal party.

So far as the first problem is concerned, it is difficult to argue that electorally or in terms of government unity and parliamentary morale, the pre-war Liberal party was a party in decline. Of course the Liberals lost heavily in the 1910 elections compared with their landslide victory in 1906; but they continued to form the governing party of England until 1915. It is true also that up to 1910 Labour had made some spectacular gains from the Liberals and (due primarily to the accession of the miners' MPs) its parliamentary strength increased. Nevertheless, during the two elections of that year and the by-elections that followed up to 1914, the Liberals successfully contained the Labour party, electorally and psychologically. P. F. Clarke therefore contends that the Liberal party was building up strong support among the industrial working classes during the whole Edwardian period, and this was so after the emergence of 'class' politics in the early part of the century, a process more or less completed by and reflected in the elections of 1910 (**61**). The workers' recognition of their class interests thus drove them not away from but towards the Liberal party, and this was a response to the 'New Liberalism' of the period, based on state-sponsored social reform, typified by the work of ministers like Lloyd George and Churchill and the ideas of the circle around C. P. Scott of the *Manchester Guardian*. 'The Liberal revival', writes Clarke, 'gave evidence of its scale in 1906 and its durability in 1910'; nor was there any reason to suppose that it would not continue. As one Liberal MP wrote: 'The present Government has beaten the record of all modern Governments by winning three general elections. We believe that we shall win the fourth, when it comes along' (**61**).

If then the Liberal party was in reasonably good health before 1914, it has been strongly argued by some historians that the new and unforeseen factor that heralded its decline was the impact of the First World War. This was so from two points of view. The war revealed the incompatibility between the Liberal ethic and the practical demands of modern warfare; and out of this ideological clash followed a political split between Asquith and Lloyd George which by 1918 left the party weakened and disheartened, unfit to face the challenges of the postwar world. These views are implicit in Trevor Wilson's *Downfall of the Liberal Party* with its famous metaphor of the First World War as a 'rampant omnibus' which knocked down and ran over the Liberal party. 'The outbreak of the First World War', he writes, 'initiated a process of disintegration in the Liberal party which by 1918 had reduced it to ruins' (**94**). The same point has been put more extravagantly by Roy Douglas: 'What shattered the Liberal Party was not the vital issues of principle which divided Liberals . . . but rather a series of largely accidental factors which arose both during and after the war' (**69**).

A number of recent writers, however, are profoundly sceptical about the whole notion of the First World War as an initiator of fundamental social and political change. On the specific issue of Liberal decline it has been argued that, far from the war acting as the initiator, social and economic forces were already at work in late Edwardian society that were undermining the bases of Liberal political power. The point has been put most cogently by Henry Pelling, who writes that the decline of the Liberal party 'was the result of long-term social and economic changes which were simultaneously uniting Britain geographically and dividing her inhabitants in terms of class' (**88**). He emphasises in particular the growing urbanisation, the increasing concentration of British industry as a whole, and incipient economic problems within specific industries such as coal-mining. These trends, together with the rising cost of living and the influence of left-wing ideas, were bound to lead to an increased class-consciousness among sections of the industrial working class, which would slowly but inexorably turn them away from the Liberal towards the Labour party. There are for Pelling two outstanding examples of this process in pre-war Britain: the affiliation of the Miners' Federation of Great Britain (MFGB) to the Labour party in 1909, which formally destroyed the long-standing link between the miners and the Liberal party; and the extraordinary growth of trade unionism between 1910 and 1914 from about two-and-a-half to over four million, about half of whom were affiliated to the Labour party.

Other labour historians have attempted to show in detail the importance of these general factors for the prospects of the two radical parties in the pre-war decade. Roy Gregory, in his study of the miners, has shown how by the eve of the First World War the Lib/Lab alliance was beginning to crumble in a number of coalfields owing to growing divisions between the Liberal employers and their workforce over pay and conditions of work, and the influence of a new generation of socialist union officials (**29**). In 1914 the Miners' Federation was planning to sponsor more Labour candidates against the Liberals at the next election, and if that trend continued there was the prospect of all the miners' seats being lost to the Liberals, as indeed they were after 1918. Similarly, Ross McKibbin has argued in a more general way, that Edwardian England saw the rise of 'an acutely developed working-class consciousness' which was reflected, not in ideology nor in the tiny Parliamentary Labour Party, but in trade union growth (**39**). It was the trade unions who financed the Labour party and sustained the national network of local trade clubs and labour parties on which Labour's electoral organisation was based. The Liberals had no comparable direct link with a massive working-class movement. It was this growing working-class consciousness that represented the greatest threat to the hegemony of the Liberal party, since it led to 'a growing feeling in the country that the Liberal Party was no longer the party of the working classes, but that in some perceived if indefinable way the Labour Party was' (**39**). For though the Edwardian Liberals prided themselves on being a 'classless' party, representing the interests of and pursuing harmony between all classes, they were a middle-class party through and through, in leadership, organisation and ethos (**49, 62**). This was especially true at the local level where working men had always found it difficult to be accepted. This helps to account for the real decline of independent Liberalism in local politics during this period, with the consequent enhancement of Labour's power in a number of urban areas (**62, 55**).

Whether the growth of 'working-class consciousness' in pre-war England is as important as here made out is problematical – the concept itself is an elusive one. What can be asserted, however, is that when every possible allowance is made in Labour's favour, the fact still remains that the electoral results between 1910 and 1914 show no real current of opinion moving away from the Liberals towards the Labour party (**60**). Roy Douglas therefore sees not the Liberals but 'Labour in decline' during these years, and writes: 'No shred of evidence existed anywhere which might suggest that within ten years the Labour party would be forming the government of the country' (**71**). But this view ignores completely one fundamental aspect of the problem: the character of the Edwardian electoral system. For it can be argued, not that the electoral evidence of the period disproves the existence of a pro-Labour working-class consciousness, but rather that its political expression was frustrated by the constrictions of the electoral system within which it developed. That system has now been subjected to detailed scrutiny, and it is evident that it was far less democratic than previously supposed (**21, 38, 44**). It was not only that women in Edwardian England lacked the vote, but specific male groups such as paupers and living-in servants were also excluded. Moreover, owing to the archaic registration and residential qualifications, many adult males in practice failed to obtain the vote. It has been estimated, therefore, that about 40 to 45 per cent of men in pre-war England were excluded from the franchise for one reason or another; and since most of these were inevitably members of the less privileged groups, the industrial working classes did not form a majority of the Edwardian electorate. Hence the political power of the Liberal party was based not on a mass electorate but on the support of a section of the middle class and a small working-class élite. Nor, despite their radical pretensions, did the Liberal leadership make any resolute effort to get to grips with the fundamental problem of extending a limited male electorate. And one of the reasons for this, even apart from the diversionary role of suffragism, was their fear that an enlarged electorate would benefit Labour (**44**).

Hence the enormous importance of the Representation of the People Act of 1918, which (according to a recent analysis) 'was of first importance in Labour's replacing the Liberal Party as the principal party of progress' (**38**). Even though the shaping of the Act may have owed more to pre-war debate than to wartime experience, as Martin Pugh argues, its consequences were profound (**44**). By giving the vote to women over thirty and removing many of the technical restrictions on the exercise of the franchise, it trebled the electorate, from roughly seven to twenty-one million voters, and also introduced important redistribution clauses. Thus the industrial working classes became for the first time the majority in a new mass electorate. It seems probable, moreover, that it was from the new voters that Labour drew its electoral strength in the post-war world. Hence, though they retained a hard core of support from the old electoral régime, it was the inability of the Liberals to win over the new working-class voters that helps to explain their electoral recession relative to Labour after 1918. Why was this?

One reason is that the new voters had no existing predisposition to vote Liberal, and were therefore open to Labour persuasion (**24**). In this respect the Liberals perhaps also suffered through the ending of old religious issues, such as Welsh Disestablishment, which slowly weakened their traditional foothold in the 'Celtic Fringe' (**85**); and indeed through the decline of political nonconformity generally (**36**). Clearly too the split within the Liberal leadership, particularly during the 1918 coupon election, was an important factor.

The result of 1918 [wrote Herbert Gladstone looking back from the vantage point of 1924] broke the party not only in the House of Commons but in the country. Local Associations perished or maintained a nominal existence. Masses of our best men passed away to Labour. Others gravitated to Conservatism or independence. Funds were depleted and we were short of workers all over the country. There was an utter lack of enthusiasm or even zeal (**61**).

But can these profound results be attributed solely to a leadership-split within a party which could still be regarded as basically one and was reunited in 1923? The Labour party too had split during the war, and though it had nearly sixty MPs in 1918 it was not really reunited as an effective parliamentary force until 1922. It is difficult to believe, therefore, that the decline of the Liberal party can be attributed simply to these political factors. What must also be taken into account are those social and economic trends that have already been referred to (**56**).

Whatever may have been its position in Edwardian England, working-class consciousness increased markedly during the years following the outbreak of the First World War as a result of the enhanced position and prestige of labour during the war, the impact of the Russian Revolution and, in the immediate post-war years, the growing division between capital and labour in key industries (especially coal-mining) reflected in a bitter wave of industrial strife. The new power of labour was seen in another great leap forward in trade union numbers, from roughly four million in 1914 to about eight million in 1919, covering nearly half the total work force. This expansion, together with the trade union movement's own internal reorganisation and consolidation, made organised labour more powerful than it had ever been before. This mass trade union power buttressed the Labour party and gave it an established and expanding electoral base among the industrial working classes (**39**). By contrast, in an age of increased class polarisation, the Liberal party lacked any definite class basis or class appeal, and this hampered it in a variety of ways (**96**). Financially and organisationally (as we have seen in some detail) it was in a much weaker position than its Labour rival with its automatic subventions from the trade unions and a strongly national and centralised organisation. The introduction of its new Constitution in 1918 meant that the Labour party now had a programme which offered the masses both immediate industrial reforms and the heady vision of a socialist future (**15, 57**). But what social and economic policies had the Liberals to offer the country to rival the practical and emotional appeal of Labour? They passionately supported Free Trade − but that was a dying cause; they were not socialists − but they failed to evolve an industrial policy which could be regarded as a realistic and distinctive alternative to Labour's socialism, at least until the publication of Lloyd George's 'coloured books' in the later twenties (**58**).

Nor, in the immediate post-war years, were the Liberal leaders in a position to counteract the class appeal of the Labour party on personal grounds. Asquith, always remote from working-class experience, was now a negligible figure; while Lloyd George, because of his leadership of a Conservative-dominated Coalition and his devious industrial policies both during and after the war, had now completely lost the confidence of the British labour movement (**95**). Labour had its own charismatic leader in Ramsay MacDonald, and it was MacDonald who was able to express perfectly in his sentimental and emotional way the deep-rooted feelings of the labour movement in the 1920s (**106**). He also had a political strategy. The key to Labour advance lay, he believed, in the destruction of the Liberal party as a rival party of the Left. Labour must therefore retain the lead it had established over the Liberals in 1918 and, before they could effectively reunite, push them permanently into third place in the political stakes. Politics would then revolve around a Conservative/Labour struggle in which the Liberals could be presented as an irrelevant and dying party, and Labour as the only possible alternative government (**106**). To the consternation and bewilderment of the Liberals it was this policy of 'non-cooperation' that was applied skilfully and ruthlessly after 1918. By 1924 it had succeeded triumphantly. It is these six years then that form the key period in the decline of the Liberal party. Thereafter, with the Liberals definitely in third place and a tradition of Labour voting built up among the industrial working class, the task of the Liberal party in dislodging Labour became a heartbreaking one. Even the leadership, money, and imaginative policies of Lloyd George after 1926 could not combat the stigma that attached to the Liberals as 'a third party', as the general election of 1929 showed. Moreover, Labour's policy of war *à l'outrance* with the Liberals was one which the Conservatives themselves connived at, for if, on the one hand, it led to the destruction of the Liberals' influence among the working-class electorate, it also helped to push many middle-class voters to the Right, into the reassuring arms of Stanley Baldwin, a politician who shared with MacDonald a personal detestation of Lloyd George!

What is argued here is that the decline of the Liberal party was the result of a combination of long-term social and economic developments going back beyond 1914, with more immediate and contingent political factors operating between 1914 and 1924. This is not to suggest that the decline of the Liberal party was 'inevitable', if by inevitable we mean that nothing could possibly have happened to prevent it. Undoubtedly there were forces at work in English society in the first quarter of the twentieth century that were likely to lead to Labour's rise and the Liberals' decline. But that process might have been much slower and assumed a rather different form if slightly different political decisions had been taken by the men involved: if, for example, Asquith *had* joined Lloyd George's government in 1918, or the Liberal leaders had behaved more astutely in 1924. It is also important to realise, as Chris Cook has stressed, that the decline of the Liberal party was not a steady and continuous process, either chronologically or regionally. The decline in the great industrial and mining areas after 1918 was swift and sharp; in rural Britain it was slow and protracted and varied in time from region to region, with results that are still apparent even today (**63**). This highlights the task of the historian. Much attention, understandably, has been focused on the story of Liberal decline from the point of view of 'high politics'; very little (except for the outstanding work of Kenneth Morgan on Wales) on its regional or local aspect (**41, 82, 85**). It is only from detailed study at that level that further illumination can come.

Part Four: Documents

document 1
Asquith's Cabinet in 1911

Charles Hobhouse was appointed to the Cabinet in 1910 (as Chancellor of the Duchy of Lancaster and later Postmaster-General) and served until the formation of the Coalition in May 1915. As the following extract (and **doc. 3a**) *shows, his Diary is an important and vivid record of its proceedings seen through the eyes of a junior member of the right of the party.*

13 August 1911
After practically a year's experience in Cabinet, I note the following characteristics of my colleagues.

Asquith, the Prime Minister, carries naturally great weight, and everybody likes him, and has great admiration for his intellect and for the ease and rapidity of transacting business, and his extraordinary quickness in seizing the right point in any case. On the other hand he has little courage; he will adopt the views of A with apparent conviction and enthusiasm, but if the drift of opinion is against A he will find an easy method of throwing him over. He is nearly always in favour of the last speaker, and I have never seen him put his back to the wall.

Ed. Grey is clear, narrow, obstinate when convinced of the soundness of his case, but convincible up to that point. He carries great weight in Cabinet, and is apt at finding solutions of difficulties, very conciliatory, and with plenty of humour.

Haldane is a dangerous man, subtle, a good friend to his followers, but tricky and not to be trusted. He carries great weight with Asquith and I think with no one else except perhaps Grey.

Ll. George has humour – great quickness of thought, and a wonderful power of managing men for a short time. He knows no meaning in the words *truth* or *gratitude*. Asquith is afraid of him, he knows it, but likes and respects Asquith. He is a little afraid of Grey – and of no one else, and treats Winston Churchill like he would a favourite and spoilt naughty boy. He has a genuine dislike of plutocracy, some regard for squirearchy and affection for the peasant, but especially the Welsh one.

Morley is useful in keeping us to constitutional precedents, and as both George and Churchill have some veneration for him, he acts as a useful check on them. He threatens resignation twice a week, and will never go till the Govt. does.

Churchill is ill mannered, boastful, unprincipled, without any redeeming qualities except his amazing ability and industry. I doubt his courage to desert during a victorious cruise, but he would, without hesitation, desert a sinking ship.

The Diaries of Charles Hobhouse (6).

document 2

The formation of the first Coalition

The first letter, Bonar Law's 'ultimatum' of 17 May, shows the collusion between himself, Asquith and Lloyd George over the formation of the first Coalition. The second letter is an important piece of evidence on the real role of Lloyd George during the crisis.

(a)

Lansdowne House,
Berkeley Square, W.
17th May, 1915.

Dear Lloyd George,

I enclose copy of the letter.

You will see we have altered it to the extent that we do not definitely offer Coalition but the substance is the same.

Yours sincerely,
A. Bonar Law.

Lansdowne House,
17th May, 1915.

Dear Mr Asquith,

Lord Lansdowne and I have learnt with dismay that Lord Fisher has resigned, and we have come to the conclusion that we cannot allow the House to adjourn until this fact has been made known and discussed.

We think that the time has come when we ought to have a clear statement from you as to the policy which the Government intend to pursue. In our opinion things cannot go on as they are, and some change in the constitution of the Government seems to us inevitable if it is to retain a sufficient measure of public confidence to conduct the War to a successful conclusion.

The situation in Italy makes it particularly undesirable to have anything in the nature of a controversial discussion in the House of Commons at present, and if you are prepared to take the necessary steps to secure the object which I have indicated, and if Lord Fisher's resignation is in the meantime postponed, we shall be ready to keep silence now. Otherwise I must to-day ask you whether Lord Fisher has resigned, and press for a day to discuss the situation arising out of his resignation.

Yours, etc.,
A. Bonar Law.

David Lloyd George, *War Memoirs* (**8**), I, p. 137.

(**b**)   10, Downing Street, S.W.
25th May, 1915.

My dear Lloyd George,

I cannot let this troubled and tumultuous chapter in our history pass without letting you know what incalculable help and support I have found in you all through. I shall never forget your devotion, your unselfishness, your powers of resource, and what is (after all) the best of things, your self-forgetfulness.

These are the rare things which make the squalor and drudgery of politics, with its constant revelations of the large part played by petty and personal motives, endurable, and give to this drabness the lightning streak of nobility.

I thank you with all my heart,

Always yours affectionately,
H. H. Asquith.

David Lloyd George, *War Memoirs*, (**8**), I, pp. 144–5.

document 3

The Liberals and the crisis

The first extract well illustrates the bewilderment and consternation aroused among his colleagues by Asquith's secret and sudden agreement to form a Coalition with the Conservatives. The second, from the diary of MacCallum Scott, a radical Liberal backbencher, shows how the Prime Minister still retained his touch in handling the parliamentary party in a very tricky political situation.

(**a**)   *17 May 1915*
On Monday after questions I went into McKenna's room at H. of C.

and found him and Geo. Lambert in earnest conversation. I went out, but McK. followed me to my room and said that on Thursday (or Friday) night Lord Fisher came to him bringing 2 notes, one for W. S. C. and one for the P. M. saying that he could not continue at the Admiralty if W. S. C. remained as First Lord. McK. had done all he could to persuade him to alter his mind, but failed, and the notes were dispatched. On Sunday he had seen both the P.M. and Ll. G. The latter did not see the seriousness of Fisher's resignation, but was convinced later that W. S. C. could not stay. While we were talking Bonham Carter came in, his face as grey as possible, with a circulation box, which I opened. Inside was about half a quarto sheet of manuscript from the P. M. intimating that in order to prevent an acrimonious and damaging discussion on the supply of munitions he had decided to request the resignation of his colleagues so that the Govt. might be reconstituted on a broader basis. Some perfunctory words were added that it gave him the deepest pain to part, even temporarily from devoted and loyal colleagues. This precious document was as unexpected by McK. as by myself. . . . It seems that after leaving me McK. had picked up W. R. and they had gone together to the F. O. to see Grey. The latter had heard absolutely nothing of these doings, was deeply hurt at the concealment practised, and at once wrote to Asquith, bidding him for the sake of Italian intervention to keep all secrecy until after Thursday. Just then Haldane came in and was asked if he had heard the news, 'No, where from, the Dardanelles?' 'No, from Downing St,' and on being told nearly fell over his chair. As a result of Grey's note we received while we were speaking a second 'circulation', enjoining us to keep these events to ourselves and to continue the administration of our offices. We gathered that the request for resignation was decided on just before question time today, and written without consulting anyone except probably Ll. G. The P. M. had not been to see the King.

The Diaries of Charles Hobhouse (**6**).

(**b**)   *19 May 1915*

Asquith announced today that the Government was under reconstruction – personal and political. Pringle and Hogge and I put down an amendment to reduce the Whitsuntide adjournment from 3 weeks to 1 week. Afterwards we attended a scratch party meeting with Whittaker in the chair. Whittaker spoke very strongly against a coalition. Then Pringle announced an amendment and moved that the meeting support it. Holt supported. Leif Jones and Russell Rea and Murray Mac-

Donald opposed. They all took the party line that the Prime Minister owed some explanation to his party – ought to take his party into his confidence. They wanted to have it out with him but they could not attack the coalition in the House – it had gone too far for that, and they strongly deprecated Pringle's motion as a vote of no confidence. Just then Asquith was fetched by Gulland who had heard how things were shaping. Asquith spoke with deep feeling – his voice husky and his face twitching. He looked old and worried. He flung himself on our mercy. Within a week a wholly new situation had been revealed to him. There had been unexpected disclosures which had taken them wholly by surprise. He could not reveal the truth to us yet without imperilling national safety.

But the situation was of the gravest kind. Coalition became inevitable. He had no desire to retain office – he would not do it without our confidence. He was ready to resign tonight. It was not pleasant to go into harness with men who were the bitter enemies of everything he held dearest in public life – still less to part even temporarily from old friends and colleagues. He asked for our confidence – he would not let us down. He appealed to us not to have any discussion in the House, at the present stage. It would be disastrous. He could but suggest, he feared he was saying too much, that the intervention of neutrals hung in the balance and it was only by their intervention that the war could be brought to a successful conclusion. The meeting gave him an overpowering ovation.

From the *Diary of J. MacCallum Scott*, quoted in (**32**), pp. 275–6.

document 4
The formation of the Lloyd George government

The first three extracts from the correspondence of the party leaders illustrate key stages in the formation of the Lloyd George Ministry. Asquith's view of Lloyd George in the first letter may be contrasted with his earlier view in doc. 2b. The last extract gives an outsider's view of the crisis – but an intensely partisan one, since Frances Stevenson was not only Lloyd George's Private Secretary but also his mistress.

(**a**)
The Wharf, Sutton Courtney,
Berks.
November 26, 1916.

My dear Bonar Law,
    What follows is intended for your eyes alone.

I fully realise the frankness and loyalty with which you have put forward the proposal embodied in your paper note. But under present conditions, and in the form in which it is presented, I do not see my way to adopt it . . .

As to Lloyd George, you know as well as I do both his qualities and his defects. He has many qualities that would fit him for the first place, but he lacks the one thing needful – he does not inspire trust. . . . Here, again, there is one construction, and one only, that could be put on the new arrangement – that it has been engineered by him with the purpose, not perhaps at the moment, but as soon as a fitting pretext could be found, of his displacing me.

In short, the plan could not, in my opinion, be carried out without fatally impairing the confidence of loyal and valued colleagues, and undermining my own authority.

I have spoken to you with the same frankness that you use to me, and which I am glad to say had uniformly marked our relations ever since the Coalition was formed. Nor need I tell you that, if I thought it right, I have every temptation (especially now) to seek relief from the intolerable daily burden of labour and anxiety.

Yours very sincerely,
H. H. Asquith.

From Beaverbrook (**17**), I, pp. 153–5.

(**b**)   10, Downing Street, S.W.
December 4, 1916.

My dear Lloyd George,

Thank you for your letter of this morning.

The King gave me to-day authority to ask and accept the resignations of all my colleagues, and to form a new Government on such lines as I should submit to him. I start, therefore, with a clean slate.

The first question which I have to consider is the constitution of the new War Committee.

After full consideration of the matter in all its aspects, I have come decidedly to the conclusion that it is not possible that such a Committee could be made workable and effective without the Prime Minister as its Chairman. I quite agree that it will be necessary for him, in view of the other calls upon his time and energy, to delegate from time to time the chairmanship to another Minister as his representative and *locum tenens*; but (if he is to retain the authority, which corresponds to his responsibility, as Prime Minister) he must continue to be, as he always has been, its permanent President. I am satisfied, on reflection, that any other arrangement (such, for instance, as the one which I indicated to you in my letter of to-day) would be found in experience impracticable, and incompatible with the retention of the Prime Minister's final and supreme control . . .

I have only to say, in conclusion, that I am strongly of opinion that the War Committee (without any disparagement of the existing Committee, which, in my judgment, is a most efficient body, and has done, and is doing, invaluable work) ought to be reduced in number; so that it can sit more frequently, and overtake more easily the daily problems with which it has to deal. But in any reconstruction of the Committee, such as I have, and have for some time past had, in view, the governing consideration, to my mind, is the special capacity of the men who are to sit on it for the work which it has to do.

That is a question which I must reserve for myself to decide.

Yours very sincerely,
H. H. Asquith.

From Lloyd George (**8**), I, pp. 591–2.

(**c**)

War Office,
Whitehall, S.W.
December 5, 1916.

Mr Dear Prime Minister,

I have received your letter with some surprise. On Friday I made proposals which involved not merely your retention of the Premiership, but the supreme control of the War, whilst the executive functions, subject to that supreme control, were left to others. I thought you then received these suggestions favourably. In fact, you yourself proposed that I should be the chairman of this Executive Committee, although, as you know, I never put forward that demand. On Saturday you wrote me a letter in which you completely went back on that proposition. You sent for me on Sunday and put before me other proposals; these proposals you embodied in a letter to me written on Monday:

'The Prime Minister to have supreme and effective control of war policy;

The Agenda of the War Committee will be submitted to him; its chairman will report to him daily; he can direct it to consider particular topics or proposals and all its conclusions will be subject to his approval or veto. He can, of course, at his own discretion attend meetings of the Committee.'

These proposals safeguarded your position and power as Prime Minister in every particular. I immediately wrote you accepting them 'in letter and in spirit.' It is true that on Sunday I expressed views as to the constitution of the Committee, but these were for discussion. To-day you have gone back on your own proposals.

I have striven my utmost to cure the obvious defects of the War Committee without overthrowing the Government. As you are aware, on several occasions during the last two years I have deemed it my duty to express profound dissatisfaction with the Government's method of conducting the War. Many a time, with the road to victory open in front of us, we have delayed and hesitated whilst the enemy were erecting barriers that finally checked the approach. There has been delay, hesitation, lack of forethought and vision. I have endeavoured repeatedly to warn the Government of the dangers, both verbally and in written memoranda and letters, which I crave your leave now to publish if my action is challenged; but I have either failed to secure decisions or I have secured them when it was too late to avert the evils. The latest illustration is our lamentable failure to give timely support to Roumania.

I have more than once asked to be released from my responsibility for a policy with which I was in thorough disagreement, but at your urgent personal request I remained in the Government. I realise that when the country is in peril of a great war, Ministers have not the same freedom to resign on disagreement. At the same time I have always felt – and felt deeply – that I was in a false position inasmuch as I could never defend in a whole-hearted manner the action of a Government of which I was a member. We have thrown away opportunity after opportunity, and I am convinced, after deep and anxious reflection, that it is my duty to leave the Government in order to inform the people of the real condition of affairs, and to give them an opportunity, before it is too late, to save their native land from a disaster which is inevitable if the present methods are longer persisted in. As all delay is fatal in war, I place my office without further parley at your disposal . . .

> Yours sincerely,
> D. Lloyd George.

From Lloyd George (**8**), I, pp. 593–4.

(**d**) *November 30th 1916*
B. Law, Carson & D. have drawn up a memo on the reconstitution of the War Committee & its new powers, & a copy of it has been sent to

the P.M. If the P.M. refuses to accept it, then there will be a smash. The only weak spot is Bonar Law, who cannot make up his mind to strike. If D. strikes alone, it will mean his forming an opposition, but if he & Bonar strike together it will mean the smashing up of the Government. Asquith has great influence over Bonar, & is using it to his full advantage. D. says that the P.M. is absolutely devoid of all principles except one – that of retaining his position as Prime Minister. He will sacrifice everything except No. 10 Downing St. D. says he is for all the world like a Sultan with his harem of 23, using all his skill and wiles to prevent one of them from eloping. However the whole country is pretty sick of him. We are receiving countless anxious letters from all parts of the country, urging D. to take over affairs. He seems to be the only one in whom the people have any confidence, & I am certain that if he were to resign now he would have the backing of the whole country.

Quoted in Taylor, ed. (**11**).

document 5

The 'coupon election'

This letter from F. E. Guest to Lloyd George shows clearly the origins of and reasons for the 'coupon election' fought by Lloyd George in December 1918 in collaboration with the Conservatives. 'Freddie' Guest was the Coalition Liberal Chief Whip.

13 July 1918

Dear Prime Minister,
    After very careful consideration the Committee arrived at the following unanimous recommendations:

1 That a form of agreement with the Conservatives as to candidates should be prepared and signed without delay.
2 That immediate steps be taken to draw up an agreed programme which should be jointly signed as a basis of policy.
3 That a general statement of policy should be made public by the Prime Minister at a favourable opportunity, leaving the fuller and more explicit pronouncement until some appropriate moment after the decision had been made as to the date of the General Election.

A Sub-Committee was formed, as follows:
                    Dr Addison (Chairman)
                    Lord Cawley
                    Dr Shakespeare

Sir Hamar Greenwood
Mr Munro
The Chief Whip (ex officio)

in order to prepare the outlines of a Programme which would be acceptable to your Liberal colleagues and supporters. . . .

From the opinions expressed yesterday, I am fortified in my view that your chief considerations now should be:

1 How to safeguard your supporters in the House of Commons;

and

2 To enable us to get candidates into the field.

As far as the *electors* are concerned you may rest assured that a *big majority* will vote for your continued leadership during the War.

I therefore trust that you will, at any rate, take some preliminary steps to force the pace.

With reference to the *'khaki' voters*, especially abroad, could not something be done to ensure their vote being cast for the Government?

Quoted in Wilson (**94**), pp. 151–2.

document 6

Asquith in 1921

The writer is C. P. Scott, the great Liberal editor of the Manchester Guardian, *who was generally a critical admirer of Lloyd George.*

What struck me most about Asquith was his immobility. He had not moved – did not really know about things; could not believe that George was really keen about the Irish question and dead set on settling it; thought if he did it would do him no good. Ireland was unpopular, he was in favour of giving her fiscal autonomy, but thought people here would resent it if her taxes were lower than ours. Had advocated great concessions to Ireland because he thought them right, but had never deluded himself as to the unpopularity of this. He had not seen de Valera and knew nothing as to his real temperament and outlook. Again thought nothing of Austen Chamberlain, wholly ignoring his sterling qualities and setting him down as a poor creature. So also of George, he could see no good in him or anything he did. All the time he laid down the law with great positiveness. Altogether a somewhat querulous and very old old man.

In my last words with Maclean at the House he said suddenly, as if liberating his soul, "For myself I have done with Lloyd George. I could never work with him or under him". I said "that's all right for you. My position is quite different. George seems to like to keep in touch with me as representing, I suppose, a certain type of Liberalism. Whatever one may think of him he is a great force. Whatever I may count for it's my business to turn that force as far as I can to good ends". He did not dissent but said "Do you go further and call him not only a great force but a great man". At least I said he will occupy a considerable place in history . . .

Of Asquith himself, though entirely loyal, [Maclean] said that he had evidence that he was not gaining but losing ground in the country. He had missed a great and unique opportunity by his failure to make any figure in Parliament since his return. Was it I asked consideration for him (Maclean) or indolence. Something of both said Maclean, but he evidently thought that the first was only a cover for the second.

The Political Diaries of C. P. Scott 1911–28 (**13**), pp. 400–1.

document 7

The downfall of Lloyd George, 1922

Tom Jones was a civil servant who served Lloyd George (and three other prime ministers in the 1920s) and particularly enjoyed his confidence, partly because he was a fellow Welshman.

19 October 1922

When I reached No. 10 about 5.15 the P.M. was closeted with his Liberal colleagues in the Cabinet room. I went back to Whitehall Gardens and when I returned to No. 10 sometime after 6.00 the Liberal members were coming away with very gloomy faces. Macnamara spoke to me remarking 'This is a very sad business and with a bad winter in front of us the power of the communists will grow rapidly'. Sir William Sutherland came along and said: 'The P.M. would never believe that there were Ministers who sat at the same table with him who went to secret cabals to conspire at his downfall. He has been told so repeatedly. Perhaps he will now believe it.' Lord Riddell was in the Private Secretary's room. He said the fatal day had been the day at San Remo when, against the advice of Foch and Henry Wilson, Lloyd George had listened to Venizelos with his promise of Greek troops for Smyrna. As for Bonar Law he was probably in the position described in an old *Punch* cartoon in which Lord Russell having been knocking at the door of the Cabinet room suddenly finds it open and runs round the corner to hide saying to himself 'Must I really go in?' Presently the P.M. came out of the Cabinet room and saw me and said in Welsh 'Rhyddid', i.e. 'Freedom', adding 'Don't go away, I want a yarn with you'. So I stayed on and later on went into the Cabinet room and found him in excellent spirits. I told him we had been misled about the Newport election. He said that the dispute in Ebbw Vale and the speeches of Evan Davies M. P. had a good deal to do with the Labour policy and that the moment he had learned the result of the Newport election and heard definitely this morning that Bonar was going to the meeting he had told Stamfordham that he would be resigning in the course of the day.

From Jones (**7**), pp. 211–12.

document 8

Liberal reunion 1923

H. A. L. Fisher, the historian, had served as President of the Board of Education under Lloyd George. This extract from his Diary well illustrates the excitement and air of expectation in the Liberal ranks on Lloyd George's return from America, and the prospect of Liberal reunion.

9 November 1923
Go to meet L. G. at Waterloo on his way back from America. Huge crowds at station. The Welshmen sing Welsh hymns and national songs . . . The crush on the platform so great that I cannot shake hands with him. However a row of motor cars is waiting to take us to 35 Lowndes Square, where we are to dine with Mond. The crowd is so great that for a quarter of an hour we can only just crawl. Dinner at Mond's – I sit next L. G. . . . . After dinner we talk politics. Mond had been seeing the Asquiths and found them both favourable to Liberal reunion. Mond says that Asquith will meet L. G. and it's arranged that they should meet next week. If possible on Monday. Mond to go down to the Wharfe on Sunday for the purpose of making the arrangements. L. G. asks us all 'Shall he meet Asquith?' Opinion unanimous for it. L. G. says that we can't win (because of the split vote) but Liberals may be the majority. As it is the country suffers greatly from having as Leader of the Opposition a man [MacDonald] who has had no Cabinet experience . . . L. G. observes of the crowd that met him, 'There seems to be a fiercer political feeling than I have seen in England for some time'.

Quoted in Campbell (**98**), p. 72.

Lloyd George and the first Labour government, 1924

Despite the breezy tone, Lloyd George's realism and shrewdness come over in the letter to his daughter. Megan Lloyd George was herself later a Liberal and subsequently a Labour MP. The second extract is interesting for its hints of Lloyd George's later reports on industrial policy, and its comments on Asquith.

(a)   *To Megan Lloyd George, 4 February 1924*
What changes are taking place. A socialist govt. actually in power. But don't get uneasy about your investments or your antiques. Nothing will be removed or abstracted. They have come in like a lamb. Will they go out like a lion? Who knows? For the present "their tameness is shocking to me". They are all engaged in looking as respectable as lather & blather will make them. They are out to soothe ruffled nerves. When you return you will find England quite unchanged. Ramsay is just a fussy Baldwin – & no more.

The Liberals were bound to turn Baldwin out & the King was bound to call Ramsay in & we are all bound to give him a chance. That is the situation.

Lloyd George Family Letters (**9**), p. 202.

(b)   *27 April, Sunday*
A car met me at Guildford and took me to Churt by about 10.30. Mrs Carey Evans there, Miss Sophie Rees (Private Secretary to Dame Margaret), and L.G. L.G. and I talked from 11 till 1, it being too wet to walk out. He began by telling me of his visit to his constituents in Carnarvonshire. Excellent meetings, lots of young people, and a growing opposition to Labour among the Liberals. Throughout our talk he was plainly preoccupied with the relations of the Liberal Party in the House and in the country to the Labour Party, and clearly willing to be on good terms with Labour. He did not want office – he had had his fling – but he was out to help. The Labour programme was more timid and prudent than his own pre-War campaign. They were doing nothing about the land, and they would muddle Housing. I suggested they would get lots of 'kudos' from the Budget which is to be introduced on Tuesday. He replied 'Only if it is a bold Budget and if it leads to a first-class controversy.' Otherwise he did not think there would be many votes in it. He was much impressed with Wheatley's emotional eloquence: 'I had a lump in my throat when he spoke the other day on evictions.' I suggested that what the Liberal Party needed was a

coherent constructive policy which could be distinguished from Socialism and Toryism. He said that a number of Committees were at work shaping out such a policy, and after lunch he gave me a Memorandum by Philip Kerr, written for one of these Committees, in which P. K. urged nationalisation of minerals and a substantial increase in the workers' participation in the control of the industry. There is a Committee on Electrification also. 'But', he went on, 'the trouble is that when you have got a policy ready and Asquith launches it, it will freeze on his lips; all kindling warmth and hope will die out of it; he will present it accurately, but without sympathy.' He liked Asquith, worked cordially with him, but as a leader he was too coldly intellectual.

From Jones (**7**), pp. 277–8.

document 10

The Liberals and the General Strike

Both extracts (though obviously partisan accounts) show the importance and political courage of Lloyd George's stand over the General Strike. As we know, it was he not Asquith who won the 'fight for his political life'.

(**a**) *May 15th 1926*
D. has had an anxious fortnight during the General Strike. 'The Nine Days' Blunder'. He took a line peculiarly his own, and for this he has been howled at by the Tories, and cold-shouldered by all the Liberals with the exception of Kenworthy, Hutchison and Garro Jones. But he stuck to his guns, unpopular though it made him. He criticised the Government for having dallied and dawdled when resolute action might have avoided the strike – and for this was called unpatriotic, because he did not support the Government wholeheartedly in the emergency – an emergency which ought never to have happened.

The Labour people are pleased with him. He has proved more of a friend to them than Ramsay Macdonald, who got cold feet, or even J. H. Thomas, who showed up very badly, and who D. thinks is broken as a result of the strike. When D. spoke in the House the first week of the strike, the Labour people cheered him. Hartshorn overheard Ramsay Macdonald say to those next to him, 'There they go, the b . . . . . fools, cheering him again.' The Labour Party have been getting more and more friendly to D. all the session. In the fight over the Economy Bill he led the Opposition, and they practically acknowledged it, and the last time D. got up to speak during the

Debate the whole Labour Party cheered him.

D. is pursuing a definite policy, and the strike has helped him in forwarding it, though it has had the effect of making him temporarily unpopular in the country, whereas there is no doubt that Baldwin has temporarily made strides.

(b)   *May 21st 1926*

A new development. Last night D. dined with me. I left the office about 6.30. & he was to come on at 7.30. He was a little late, & came in very excitedly, so that I could see something had happened. He said to me: 'I have been expelled from the Party.' And handed me Oxford's letter to read. I read it & remarked that it was clearly a letter intended for D.'s resignation. It was a shock to both of us, & I don't think we discussed it very connectedly, or at least definitively, but rather speculated as to the influences which had led up to it. In brief it was obvious that the Old Gang thought D.'s luck and popularity were down as a result of the strike, and that this was a time to get rid of him. Dirty work. The Asquith women are of course at the bottom of it. My chief concern last night was to get D. into a calm frame of mind. It was a blow for him − rather a cruel one. It faced him with a crisis the like of which he had not quite experienced before. He has now before him a fight for his political life.

Quoted in Taylor, ed. (**11**).

document 11

'We can conquer unemployment'

This is an extract from the manifesto issued under the above title on which the Liberals fought − and lost − the general election of 1929, which was itself based on the Liberal Yellow Book, Industry and the Nation. *The influence of Keynesian economic ideas is clearly apparent.*

WORK FOR THE WORKLESS, NOW

We felt it advisable to refer thus briefly to these numerous directions in which work of national development is called for outside of the six groups upon which attention is here mainly concentrated; and to point out that whilst we consider this policy of national development to be of paramount immediate importance, it forms only part of a larger whole. Having done this, we return to our main theme, namely, the provision of work for the workless, now.

Adopting a reasoned and balanced view throughout, and stating the details for consideration, we have outlined proposals which we believe will provide a great volume of useful employment over a period of years. In particular, we have shown how by work of necessary development in six chosen spheres alone, work can be directly provided in the following estimated proportions, the figures summarizing the effect of the proposals given in detail above . . .

INDIRECT EFFECTS ON EMPLOYMENT

In all this, so far, we have taken no account of the large increase in employment everywhere resulting indirectly from the addition to the national purchasing power represented by the wages of those workers directly employed in this way. The income of every one of these will have increased twice or thrice; and this will be reflected at once in a corresponding increase in expenditure on food, clothing, boots, housing, travelling, entertainment, and other amenities. As a result, a stimulus will be given to the whole of the industry and commerce of the country, reflected, in turn, in increased employment.

Again, we have included in our figures those employed in industries directly supplying the materials to be used in our national development scheme, but not those less directly affected. Thus, while we have included those working on roads, we have not included those making the additional vehicles which in consequence will come upon those roads; those building houses, but not those making the furniture and carpets for those houses; those installing electric generating plant and cables, but not those manufacturing the lamps and fittings which will be used at the ends of those cables.

After taking all these things into account, we have every confidence that **within three months of a Liberal Government being in power, large numbers of men at present unemployed could be engaged on useful work of national development; and that within twelve months the numbers unemployed would be brought down to normal proportions.**

Statistical evidence shows the normal pre-war percentage of unemployment to have been some 4.7 per cent. Applied to the present insured population this represents about 570,000.

We should not, of course, rest satisfied with that, but should resume that policy which Liberalism was pursuing up to the outbreak of war, designed to reduce and mitigate still further the burden of normal unemployment.

To summarize: **Unemployment is industrial disorganization. It is brought to an end by new enterprise, using capital to employ labour. In the present stagnation the Government must supply** that initiative which will help to set going a great progressive movement.

Lloyd George, *We Can Conquer Unemployment.*

document 12

The Liberal Parliamentary Party in 1931

Sir Archibald Sinclair was appointed Chief Whip in November 1930 on the resignation of Sir George Hutchison who was opposed to Lloyd George's policy of cooperation with Labour. His letter shows the disunion and confusion into which the Liberal Parliamentary Party had now fallen. Sinclair himself resigned in disgust within a year. In 1935 he was elected leader of the Liberal party.

Broadly speaking the position is that the vast majority of the Party are working well together under Mr Lloyd George's leadership.... Nevertheless there are certain members of the Party – and among them some of the best known Liberals in the country such as Simon and Hutchison – who are definitely bent on turning out the Government and making an agreement with the Conservatives, and they are in a position to ensure those who follow them that they will have no Tory opponent at the next General Election. They constitute a nucleus of disloyalty and disaffection in the party; their interventions in debate and constant opposition in the division lobby weaken the influence of the party in the House of Commons, while their criticism of our policy as unprincipled as well as unwise bewilders and discourages our supporters in the country....

In Mr Lloyd George's opinion, our chief concern must be to carry out in this Parliament the mandate which we received at the last election from over five million electors and obviously this can only be done by agreement with the Labour Party. The view, therefore, to which he is now inclining is that we should endeavour to come to some agreement with the Labour Party covering India, Disarmament, Free Trade, National Development and Unemployment, and Electoral Reform; and, while reserving our right as an independent party to criticize or oppose the Government on matters not covered by the agreement, assure them of our general support so long as the agreed policy is being carried out.

Mr Lloyd George has no desire to drum any Liberals out of the Party, and it is obvious that members who have been returned to Parliament as candidates of Liberal Associations are entitled to receive the Whip. Nevertheless there would be an advantage if we knew that there were 40 or 45 members on whose loyalty and cooperation we could definitely rely.

If some definite and advantageous understanding could be reached with the Labour Government on this basis, we should be able to get a great deal of useful work done in this Parliament during the next two years, and we should be able to face the electors with much better prospects at the end of that time than we could in the existing circumstances.

If, on the other hand, the Party refuse to support any such arrangement or if we fail to come to terms with the Government, there would be a great deal to be said for a General Election in the near future.

Sinclair to H. A. L. Fisher, 20 March 1931, quoted in (**98**), pp. 286–7.

Appendix: The Liberal Vote

Elections	Votes	MPs elected	Candidates	Percentage share of total vote
1906	2,757,883	400	539	49.0
1910 (Jan)	2,880,581	275	516	43.2
1910 (Dec)	2,295,888	272	467	43.9
1918 Coalition Liberal	1,455,640	133	158	13.5
Independent Liberal	1,298,808	28	253	12.1
1922 (Lloyd George) Liberal	1,673,240	62	162	11.6
(Asquith) Liberal	2,516,287	54	328	17.5
1923	4,311,147	159	453	29.6
1924	2,928,747	40	340	17.6
1929	5,308,510	59	513	23.4
1931 Liberal National (Simonites)	809,302	35	41	3.7
Liberal (Samuelites)	1,403,102	33	112	6.5
(Lloyd George) Liberal	106,106	4	7	0.5
1935	1,422,116	21	161	6.4
1945	2,248,226	12	306	9.0

Bibliography

LETTERS, DIARIES AND MEMOIRS

1   Addison, Christopher, *Politics from Within*, 2 vols, Jenkins, 1924.
2   Asquith, the Earl of Oxford and, *Memories and Reflections*, II, Cassell, 1928.
3   Asquith, Margot, *The Autobiography of Margot Asquith*, 2 vols, Butterworth, 1920.
4   Cole, Margaret, ed. *Beatrice Webb's Diaries 1912–24*, Longmans, 1952.
5   Cole, Margaret, ed. *Beatrice Webb's Diaries 1924–32* Longmans, 1956.
6   David, Edward, ed. *Inside Asquith's Cabinet. From the Diaries of Charles Hobhouse*, Murray, 1977.
7   Jones, Thomas, *Whitehall Diary, I, 1916–25*, ed. Keith Middlemass, Oxford University Press, 1969.
8   Lloyd George, David, *War Memoirs*, 2 vols, Odhams Press edn, 1938.
9   Morgan, Kenneth O. ,ed. *Lloyd George Family Letters, 1885–1936*, Cardiff University Press, 1973.
10   Samuel, Viscount *Memoirs*, Cresset Press, 1945.
11   Taylor, A. J. P. , ed. *Lloyd George. A Diary by Frances Stevenson*, Harper, 1971.
12   Webb, Beatrice, *Our Partnership*, ed. Barbara Drake and Margaret Cole, Longmans, 1941.
13   Wilson, Trevor, ed. *The Political Diaries of C. P. Scott 1911–28*, Collins, 1970.

SOCIAL AND POLITICAL DEVELOPMENT

14   Adelman, Paul, *The Rise of the Labour Party 1880–1945*, Seminar Studies in History, Longman, 1972.
15   Barker, Rodney, 'Political myth: Ramsay MacDonald and the Labour Party', *History*, lxi, 1976.

16   Bassett, R. *Nineteen Thirty-One: political crisis*, Macmillan, 1958.

17   Beaverbrook, Lord, *Politicians and the War 1914–16*, 2 vols, Butterworth, 1928.

18   Beaverbrook, Lord, *Men and Power 1917–18*, Hutchinson, 1956.

19   Beaverbrook, Lord, *The Decline and Fall of Lloyd George*, Collins,
1963: these three volumes provide an enthralling inside view of
events.

20   Beer, Samuel H. *Modern British Politics*, Faber, 1965.

21   Blewett, Neal, 'The franchise in the United Kingdom
1885–1918', *Past and Present*, xxxii, 1965: *the* seminal study.

22   Blewett, Neal, *The Peers, the Parties and the People. The general elections of 1910*, Macmillan, 1972.

23   Butler, David, and Sloman, Anne, *British Political Facts
1900–1975*, 4th edn, Macmillan, 1975.

24   Butler, David, and Stokes, Donald, *Political Change in Britain*,
Macmillan, 1969; Pelican edn, 1971: a psephological view.

25   Clarke, P. F. 'Electoral sociology of modern Britain', *History*,
lvii, 1972.

26   Cook, Chris, 'By-elections of the first Labour Government', in
By-elections in British Politics, ed. Chris Cook and John Ramsden,
Macmillan, 1973.

27   Cowling, Maurice, *The Impact of Labour 1920–1924*, Cambridge
University Press, 1971: 'high politics'.

28   Craig, F. W. S. *British General Election Manifestoes 1918–1966*,
Political Reference Publications, Chichester, 1970.

29   Gregory, Roy, *The Miners and British Politics 1906–14*, Oxford
University Press, 1968.

30   Guinn, Paul, *British Strategy and Politics 1914–18*, Oxford
University Press, 1961.

31   Halévy, Elie, *A History of the English People in the Nineteenth Century, VI, 1905–14*, Benn, 1926: still an illuminating study.

32   Hazlehurst, Cameron, *Politicians at War, July 1914 to May 1915*,
Cape, 1971.

33   Holton, Bob, *British Syndicalism 1910–14*, Pluto Press, 1976.

34   James, Robert Rhodes, *The British Revolution. British politics
1880–1939*, 2 vols, Hamish Hamilton, 1976–7: an immensely
readable but superficial work.

35   Jenkins, Roy, *Mr Balfour's Poodle*, Heinemann, 1954: the Lords'
crisis.

36   Koss, Stephen, *Nonconformity in Modern British Politics*, Batsford,
1975.

37   Marwick, Arthur, *The Deluge. British society and the First World*

War, Bodley Head, 1965; Penguin edn, 1967: war as an instrument of change.

38   Matthew, H. C. G. , McKibbin, R. I. , Kay, J. A. 'The franchise factor in the rise of the Labour Party', *English Historical Review*, cclxi, 1976: a key article for Liberal decline.

39   McKibbon, Ross, *The Evolution of the Labour Party 1910–24*, Oxford University Press, 1974: of fundamental importance for Lib/Lab relations.

40   Morgan, Kenneth O. '1902–24' in *Coalitions in British Politics*, ed. David Butler, Macmillan, 1978.

41   Morgan, Kenneth O. *Wales in British Politics 1868–1922*, University of Wales Press, 1963.

42   Mowat, Charles Loch, *Britain Between the Wars 1918–1940*, Methuen, 1955: particularly useful for social and economic history.

43   Pelling, Henry, *Social Geography of British Elections 1885–1910*, Macmillan, 1967.

44   Pugh, Martin, *Electoral Reform in War and Peace 1906–18*, Routledge, 1978.

45   Ramsden, John, 'The Newport by-election and the fall of the coalition', in *By-elections in British Politics*, ed. Chris Cook and John Ramsden, Macmillan, 1973.

46   Read, Donald, *Edwardian England 1901–15*, Harrap, 1972.

47   Roover, Constance, *Women's Suffrage and Party Politics in Britain 1866–1914*, Routledge, 1967.

48   Rosen, Andrew, *Rise up Women! The militant campaign of the Women's Social and Political Union 1903–1914*, Routledge, 1975.

49   Shannon, Richard, *The Crisis of Imperialism 1865–1915*, MacGibbon, 1974; Paladin edn, 1976.

50   Skidelsky, Robert, *Politicians and the Slump. The Labour Government of 1929–31*, Macmillan, 1967; Penguin books edn, 1970.

51   Steiner, Zara S. *Britain and the Origins of the First World War*, Macmillan, 1977.

52   Stubbs, John, 'The impact of the Great War on the Conservative Party', in *The Politics of Reappraisal 1918–1939*, ed. Gillian Peele and Chris Cook, Macmillan, 1975.

53   Taylor, A. J. P. *English History 1914–1945*, Oxford University Press, 1965.

54   Taylor, A. J. P. 'Politics in the First World War', in *Essays in English History*, Penguin Books, 1976.

55   Thompson, Paul, *Socialists, Liberals and Labour. The struggle for London 1885–1914*, Routledge, 1967.

56   Waites, B. A. 'The effect of the First World War on class and status in England 1910–20', *Journal of Contemporary History*, ii, 1976.

57   Winter, J. *Socialism and the Challenge of War*, Routledge, 1974.

THE LIBERAL PARTY

58   Bentley, Michael, 'The Liberal response to socialism 1918–29', in *Essays in Anti-Labour History*, ed. Kenneth D. Brown, Macmillan, 1974.

59   Bentley, Michael, *The Liberal Mind 1914–29*, Cambridge University Press, 1977: the Liberal party minus the politics.

60   Clarke, P. F. 'The electoral position of the Liberal and Labour Parties, 1910–1914', *English Historical Review*, xc, 1975.

61   Clarke, P. F. *Lancashire and the New Liberalism*, Cambridge University Press, 1971: a major work on pre-1914 Liberalism.

62   Cook, Chris, 'Labour and the downfall of the Liberal Party, 1906–14', in *Crisis and Controversy. Essays in honour of A. J. P. Taylor*, ed. Alan Skeed and Chris Cook, Macmillan, 1976.

63   Cook, Chris, *The Age of Alignment. Electoral politics in Britain 1922–29*, Macmillan, 1975.

64   Cook, Chris, 'A stranger death of Liberal England', in *Lloyd George, Twelve Essays*, ed. A. J. P. Taylor, Hamish Hamilton, 1971.

65   Cook, Chris, *A Short History of the Liberal Party 1900–1976*, Macmillan, 1976.

66   Dangerfield, George, *The Strange Death of Liberal England*, Constable, 1935; Paladin Books edn, 1970.

67   David, Edward, 'The Liberal Party divided 1916–1918', *The Historical Journal*, xiii, 1970.

68   Dockrill, M. L. 'Lloyd George and foreign policy before 1914', in *Lloyd George, Twelve Essays*, ed. A. J. P. Taylor, Hamish Hamilton, 1971.

69   Douglas, Roy, *History of the Liberal Party 1895–1970*, Sidgwick and Jackson, 1971.

70   Douglas, Roy, 'The background to the "Coupon" election arrangements', *English Historical Review*, lxxxvi, 1971.

71   Douglas, Roy, 'Labour in Decline 1910–14', in *Essays in Anti-Labour History*, ed. Kenneth D. Brown, Macmillan, 1974.

72   Emy, H. V. 'The Land Campaign: Lloyd George as a social reformer 1909–14', in *Lloyd George, Twelve Essays*, ed. A. J. P. Taylor, Hamish Hamilton, 1971.

73 Grigg, John, 'Liberals on trial', in *Crisis and Controversy. Essays in honour of A. J. P. Taylor*, ed. Alan Skeed and Chris Cook, Macmillan, 1976.

74 Hazlehurst, Cameron, 'Asquith as Prime Minister 1908–16', *English Historical Review*, lxxxv, 1970.

75 Hazlehurst, Cameron, 'The conspiracy myth', in *Lloyd George*, ed. Martin Gilbert, Prentice-Hall, 1968.

76 Kinnear, Michael, *The Fall of Lloyd George. The political crisis of 1922*, Macmillan, 1973.

77 Koss, Stephen, 'The destruction of Britain's last Liberal Government', *Journal of Modern History*, xl, 1968.

78 Lowe, Peter, 'The Rise to the Premiership 1914–16', in *Lloyd George, Twelve Essays*, ed. A. J. P. Taylor, Hamish Hamilton, 1971.

79 McGill, Barry, 'Asquith's predicament 1914–18', *Journal of Modern History*, xxxix, 1967.

80 Morgan, David, *Suffragists and Liberals. The politics of woman suffrage in England*, Blackwell, 1975.

81 Morgan, Kenneth O. 'Lloyd George and the historians', *The Transactions of the Honourable Society of Cymmrodorian*, Session 1971.

82 Morgan, Kenneth O. 'Cardiganshire politics: the Liberal ascendancy 1885–1923', *Ceredigion*, 1967.

83 Morgan, Kenneth O. 'Lloyd George's premiership: a study in "prime ministerial government"', *The Historical Journal*, xiii, 1970.

84 Morgan, Kenneth O. *The Age of Lloyd George: The Liberal Party and British politics 1890–1929*, Allen and Unwin, 1971.

85 Morgan, Kenneth O. 'The new Liberalism and the challenge of Labour: the Welsh experience 1885–1929', in *Essays in Anti-Labour History*, ed. Kenneth D. Brown, Macmillan, 1974.

86 Morgan, Kenneth O. 'Twilight of Welsh Liberalism: Lloyd George and the 'Wee Frees', 1918–35', *Bulletin of the Board of Celtic Studies*, xxii, 1968.

87 Morgan, Kenneth O. 'Lloyd George's stage army: The Coalition Liberals, 1918–22', in *Lloyd George, Twelve Essays*, ed. A. J. P. Taylor, Hamish Hamilton, 1971.

88 Pelling, Henry, 'Labour and the downfall of Liberalism', in *Popular Politics and Society in late Victorian Britain*, Macmillan 1968: an outstanding essay.

89 Pugh, Martin D. 'Asquith, Bonar Law and the first Coalition', *The Historical Journal*, xvii, 1974.

90 Rowland, Peter, *The Last Liberal Governments. Unfinished business 1911–14*, Barrie and Jenkins, 1971.

91 Russell, A. K. *Liberal Landslide. The general election of 1906*, David and Charles, 1973.

92 Taylor, A. J. P. 'Lloyd George: rise and fall', in *Essays in English History*, Penguin books, 1976.

93 Wilson, Trevor, 'The coupon and the British general election of 1918', *Journal of Modern History*, xxxvi 36, 1964.

94 Wilson, Trevor, *The Downfall of the Liberal Party 1914–1935*, Collins, 1966; Fontana edn, 1968.

95 Wrigley, C. J. *David Lloyd George and the British Labour Movement*, Harvester Press, 1976.

96 Wrigley, C. J. 'Liberals and the desire for working-class representatives in Battersea 1886–1922', in *Essays in Anti-Labour History*, ed. K. D. Brown, Macmillan, 1974.

BIOGRAPHIES

97 Blake, Robert, *The Unknown Prime Minister*, Eyre and Spottiswoode, 1955.

98 Campbell, John, *Lloyd George. The goat in the Wilderness*, Cape, 1977.

99 Gilbert, Martin, *Winston S. Churchill*, III 1914–1916; IV 1916–1922; V 1922–1939, Heinemann, 1971–76.

100 Grigg, John, *The Young Lloyd George*, Eyre Methuen, 1976.

101 Grigg, John, *Lloyd George: the people's champion*, Eyre Methuen, 1978: this and (**100**) form the best account of his career to 1910.

102 Harrod, Roy, *The Life of John Maynard Keynes*, Macmillan, 1951.

103 Jenkins, Roy, *Asquith*, Collins, 1964; Fontana edn, 1967.

104 Jones, Tom, *Lloyd George*, Oxford University Press, 1951: dull but worthy.

105 Koss, Stephen, *Asquith*, Allen Lane, 1976.

106 Marquand, David, *Ramsay MacDonald*, Cape, 1977: a major biography which does much to rehabilitate J. R. M.

107 Middlemass, Keith and Barnes, John, *Baldwin*. Weidenfeld, 1969: an elephantine biography.

108 Morgan, Kenneth O. *Lloyd George*, Weidenfeld and Nicolson, 1974: the most useful and balanced account.

109 Roskill, Stephen, *Hankey: man of secrets, I, 1877–1918*, Collins, 1970.

110 Rowland, Peter, *Lloyd George*, Barrie and Jenkins, 1976: ponderous.
111 Taylor, A. J. P. *Beaverbrook*, Hamish Hamilton, 1972: revealing on Beaverbrook as an historian.

ADDITIONAL

112 Crossman, R. H. S. *The Diaries of a Cabinet Minister*, 3 vols, Hamish Hamilton and Jonathan Cape, 1975–77.
113 Morgan, Kenneth O. *Consensus and Disunity. The Lloyd George Coalition Government 1918–1922*, Oxford University Press, 1979.

Index